On-Demand and Digital Printing Primer

by Howard M. Fenton

GATFPress
Pittsburgh

International Standard Book Number: 0-88362-219-X
Library of Congress Catalog Card Number: 98-74334

Printed in the United States of America
GATF Catalog No. 1328

GATF*Press* books are widely used by companies, associations, and schools
for training, marketing, and resale. Quantity discounts are available by
contacting Peter Oresick at 800/910-GATF.

GATF*Press*
Graphic Arts Technical Foundation
200 Deer Run Road
Sewickley, PA 15143-2600
Phone: 412/741-6860
Fax: 412/741-2311
Email: info@gatf.org
Internet: http://www.gatf.org

Orders to:
GATF Orders
P.O. Box 1020
Sewickley, PA 15143-1020
Phone (U.S. and Canada): 800/662-3916
Phone (all other countries): 412/741-5733
Fax: 412/741-0609
Email: gatforders@abdintl.com

TABLE OF CONTENTS

FOREWORD

A crash course in on-demand printing? Yes, that's what we have asked of Howard M. Fenton, senior technical consultant/digital technology with the Graphic Arts Technical Foundation. This book offers a short, illustrated, non-technical orientation to the field.

The aim of the GATF*Press* primer series is to communicate the essential concepts of printing processes and technologies. Other primers focus on lithography, flexography, gravure, and screen printing, and new titles are being planned.

On-Demand and Digital Printing Primer is useful to students, graphic artists, print buyers, publishers, salespeople in the graphic communications industry—to anyone who would like to know more about the printing process.

GATF*Press* is committed to serving the graphic communications community as a leading publisher of technical information. Please visit the GATF website at www.gatf.org for additional information about our resources and services.

Peter Oresick
Director
GATF*Press*

PREFACE

I would like to dedicate this work to three mentors.

My father asked me to work after school, weekends, and summers in his business. Working with Dad, I learned about integrity, business, and the importance of the entrepreneurial spirit.

Jeff Liebman hired me as a lab assistant and promoted me to a scientist. Working with Jeff I learned about the scientific method, the importance of remaining up-to-date, and neuroscience research. After a few years I had several first-authored publications in international scientific journals and had made presentations at international shows.

Frank Romano hired me to write for *TypeWorld* and make presentations at Type-X. After working with Frank I became editor of *Pre* magazine and was invited to present over 100 seminars a year for Printing Industries of America affiliates. Frank is also the co-author of our textbook *On-Demand Printing: The Revolution in Digital and Customized Printing*, and he has been instrumental in my foray into book publishing.

To all my mentors—thanks.

Howie Fenton

1 INTRODUCTION

t doesn't matter if you're a service provider or one of their customers; if you're looking for new business opportunities today you don't have to look farther than printing done with digital or on-demand printing technologies. Experts in printing, market research, and direct response agree unanimously that printing faster (digital printing) and cheaper (on-demand printing), and combining the ability to target single customers or market "one-to-one" (personalized and customized), gives digital and on-demand printing a significant competitive advantage over traditional printing. Some experts say it is the only way print production will keep pace with the personalized and customized advantages offered by on-line advertising.

In this chapter I will offer some introductory information, which will be expanded upon in subsequent chapters. The goal is to clear up any murky waters—before treading into deeper waters.

WHAT IS ON-DEMAND?

Both on-demand and digital color printing are geared for short printrun lengths, defined as runs of less than 5,000. In later chapters I will offer an in-depth definition of digital and on-demand printing; for now let's simply define these technologies as requiring:

- Pages submitted digitally (created in software such as Microsoft Word, QuarkXPress, or Adobe PageMaker)
- Pages printed digitally, using either traditional printing (offset) or copy-based technology (electrophotographic)
- Printing that is done quickly and cost efficiently

REPRESENTATIVE EQUIPMENT

The equipment usually associated with these services are either:
1) High-speed copiers/printers, such as the Xerox DocuTech or Canon Color Copier
2) Printers using copier-based technology, such as Indigo, Océ, or Xeikon-based devices (Xeikon, Agfa Chromapress, IBM InfoPrint 70, Xerox DocuColor 70)
3) Presses that burn plates on the press, such as Heidelberg direct imaging devices (QuickMaster DI, GTO-DI) and the Karat 74 from Scitex and KBA Planeta

In a recent GATF Conference on Personalized and Database Printing, Frank J. Romano, Roger K. Fawcett Distinguished Professor at the Rochester Institute of Technology, reported the following numbers of equipment installations in the United States (US) and world wide (WW).

	WW units	US units	US sites
Agfa Chromapress	400	180	110
Canon CLC 1000	3000	1000	800
IBM InfoColor	200	90	35
Indigo	950	350	190
Océ 3125C	100	20	20
Xeikon DCP	350	150	110
Xerox DocuColor 40	4500	2100	950
Xerox DocuColor 70	50	40	7

OLD VERSUS NEW

What are the advantages of these technologies over traditional long-run printing? First, the time and cost involved with the early steps in the process (makeready) are significantly reduced. Second, the time and cost of steps late in the process (binding and finishing) are less.

What is makeready? There is a lot of work required before the first acceptable page is printed by traditional printing processes. This time and effort is called "makeready."

Typical makeready includes:

- Cameras or scanners to take pictures of submitted materials
- Processing chemistry to develop the film
- Manual stripping to assemble film
- Exposing film to a metal plate
- Mounting the plate on the press
- Time and materials required to get the first good page from the press

With digital printing there is no camera, film, processing chemistry, mechanical stripping, or plates. As a result, the time and cost of makeready is reduced because you can print digital files directly onto paper.

After pages are printed they are gathered, organized, collated, and bound together. Binding can be accomplished in a number of operations to join individual pages (or signatures) together to form a book, booklet, or pamphlet. For certain kinds of printing such as catalogs and books this step can be equipment- and labor-intensive.

Imagine printing a book one page at a time. After you print each page you put them in a holding place or binding station until the entire book is completed. Only after printing each page of this several-hundred-page book can you bind them all together. This step is known as binding.

What is the difference between binding and finishing? Although often used interchangeably, binding is not the same operation as finishing. Finishing is the step that comes after binding. Finishing is a separate operation that includes cutting and stamping to "finish" the final appearance. A simple walk through a supermarket reveals the wide variety of finishing options available—boxes for consumer foods and cleansing products, plastic blister packaging, cardboard point-of-purchase displays, etc.

This distinction is important because many of the on-demand and digital printing technologies incorporate the binding procedure but not the finishing step. With digital and on-demand equipment this occurs at the last station of the output device; when done on the same device this is called "in-line" finishing, and when done on another piece of equipment it is called "off-line". Therefore the time and effort required for binding "off-line" with traditional equipment can be saved with a device that offers this capability in-line.

One final advantage comes from the ability to print shorter run lengths, resulting in lower inventory costs and less risk of obsolescence. According to *The American Heritage Dictionary*, obsolescent means "Being in the process of passing out of use or usefulness; becoming obsolete." For our purposes obsolescence simply means that the printed piece is out of date or no longer accurate.

The high costs typically associated with makeready and binding usually result in longer printruns—the longer the printrun, the less the cost per piece.

A printing run length of 2,000 pieces could result in a cost of $10 each, or $20,000; a longer run of 6,000 could result in per unit cost of $4 each, or $24,000 total. The reason for this cost difference is that the financial burden of the makeready, press time, and bindery is nearly the same. The major price difference is paper.

As a result the typical print buyer opts for the longer run length and puts the balance in storage, planning, and hoping to use the extra pages at a later date. However, in our fast-paced world with reduced turnaround times and ever-increasing digital transmission of data, those printed pieces in storage typically become out-of-date and the savings associated with the printrun becomes a mirage.

ADVANTAGE: IT'S DIGITAL AND PERSONAL

The combination of printing pages directly from your computer and the ability to customize these pages with personal information are the biggest attractions of digital printing. This means two things. First, pages are created in page-layout programs and printed directly to digital presses, akin to printing them to a local laser printer. On the other hand, the costs for these devices are nothing like a laser printer. Instead of the few-hundred-dollar price tag for an inkjet or laser printer, digital presses range in cost from $200,000 to $650,000.

A second advantage is the ability to print different names and address on different pages. Called a mail merge when sent to a laser printer, this is called personalization or customization on a digital press. By integrating database information into a "static" document you can customize or personalize those pages for specific readers.

With personalization, retailers can target specific products. By utilizing database mining and direct-mail marketing techniques lawn mower ads would only go to homeowners and diaper ads would only go to new parents.

This has significant advantages when trying to advertise or sell a product. For the advertising community this may increase the number of responses from 2% with static pages to 20% by combining variable information. According to organizations such as the Direct Marketing Association (DMA) and publications such as *Direct Magazine:*

- Broadcast (i.e., TV and radio) only returns 0.5–1%
- Personalized printed pieces (static documents with different people's names) achieve a 2–3% return rate
- Database marketing (both name and content is varied) will result in 20–50% return rates

According to these organizations the cost to generate leads with direct mail is less expensive than with other forms of media. The chart on the following page shows the media cost for each dollar of sales.

MARKET POTENTIAL

According to market research, short-run and on-demand printing markets are poised to explode. According to Charles A. Pesko

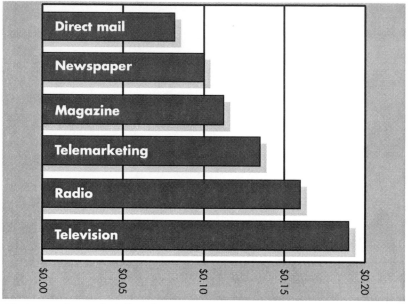

Media cost for each dollar of sales.   Source: CAPV

Ventures (CAPV), the commercial print market in 1997 was $95.2 billion, of which 48% ($45.7 billion) was short-run. This market is broken down into 38% black-and-white, 31% two- or three-color, and 31% four-color. The two- or three-color and the four-color markets combined comprise a $28.3 billion market composed of 50% four-color process and 50% two- or three-color.

Of the $28.3 billion short-run color market:

- 84% is created on traditional and digital presses (not black-and-white or color copiers)
- 76% of the work is created by commercial printers (not quick printers or in-plants)
- 50% is four-color process printing
- 48% is promotional in nature, i.e., they are nonpublishing

WHAT IS ON-DEMAND USED FOR?

There are a host of different uses or specific printed applications for these technologies—books, catalogs, in-house documents, college textbooks, insurance forms, manufacturer's manuals, and magazine reprints to name only a few.

If you ever ordered a book, you know it takes weeks to receive if it's not on the shelf. That is due to costs associated with inventory maintenance, inventory risk, and distribution. Using traditional strategies today, distribution and inventory management can account for as much as 30% of the overall cost of producing a printed product. On-demand printing can eliminate most of those costs—customers could save almost 30% by avoiding inventory maintenance, distribution issues, and associated costs for inventory risk.

College professors often create customized course notes for their students. Called Professor Publishing by Kinko's, this market niche caused the explosive growth of Kinko's shops nationwide until the company was sued for copyright infringement. However, the market remains viable and copyright issues can be overcome—University of Chicago Printing Office can print over 150 different course packs every night during enrollment and is a stickler for copyright permission.

Another advantage is that magazine reprints could be ready when the article reaches the newsstand. Today it may take weeks or months to receive reprints. Often the publisher, printer, or fulfillment company waits until there is enough demand to justify a printrun. Reprints can be made faster for less money with digital printing, and jobs can be customized for specific purposes.

Specialized catalogs of various kinds lend themselves well to the advantages of on-demand technologies, especially when combined with variable information. With electronic printing, it is possible to customize different versions. As a result you could select certain items appropriate for a specific region (i.e., winter coats for northern regions) or a specific industry (i.e., a trade show or event) to publish a custom-tailored catalog. With the advent of high-speed on-demand digital printing, this type of catalog will increase.

Catalog sales continue to grow, expected to total more than $87 billion in 1998 (a 7.7% increase over 1997 sales of almost $81 billion). The 6.1% annual growth rate forecast in the consumer catalog market from 1998 to 2003 is expected to exceed growth in total U.S. consumer sales.

Customer demand in the label printing industry, like book publishing, forms printing, and other niche markets in print production, is changing. Central to the new customer demands are shorter run lengths, higher quality, and more four-color process printing. Other factors include the increased use of multiple labels on single packages as well as an increasing popularity of data merging and variable data.

IN-PLANT PRINTERS

Equipment capabilities have been powerful enough, while the cost has fallen low enough, to allow more companies to bring printing or reprographic departments in-house. Referred to as "in-plants," market projections show that the amount of work done in-house continues to grow. Representative types of companies with in-plants are insurance companies, hospitals, and computer peripheral manufacturers.

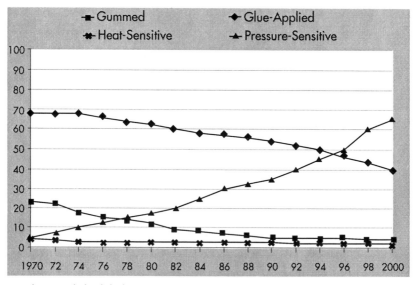

Market trends by label type.   Source: Labels & Labeling Consultancy

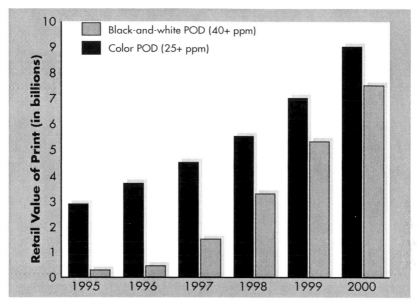

Market projection of the growth of on-demand equipment in-plants.
Source: CAPV

One of the problems in the insurance business is that the demand for forms is unpredictable, which results in long runs, storage, and possible obsolescence. Creating and storing forms electronically allows for faster and easier updates and maintaining a lower inventory.

Administrative costs in hospitals can reach 25% of operating costs, due largely to the cost of printing directories, manuals, and reports that are only needed in small quantities and have a short shelf life. These hospital forms are a perfect application for on-demand printing.

Manufacturers of computer peripherals often need very short runs and rapid updating. It used to take Tektronix twenty-eight days to update and print a manual at the cost of $120 each. With on-demand printing they can update manuals in twenty-four hours and print them for $12 each.

CHALLENGES

Along with the advantages of reduced costs, shorter runs, and increased response rate from direct marketing, there are disadvantages too. One issue is quality. Although the quality achieved with some technologies is better than with others, in general the quality of the electrophotographic devices (DocuTech, Xeikon, Indigo, Océ) does not match that of conventional offset printing. Direct-to-plate-on-press devices (i.e., Heidelberg Quickmaster DI, Omni-Adast, Scitex-KBA Planeta Karat 74) offer better quality, but do not have the variable-data printing capabilities of the electrophotographic devices.

Consumable costs are also often an issue. Most of these devices require that you buy the ink or toner from the manufacturer. This is a notoriously difficult subject to discuss with specifics because the price of consumables has been decreasing since the devices first came to market. As a point of reference, consumable costs for some of the early devices were as much as 75¢ per page.

When the color machines first began to hit the market there where serious reliability problems. Early adopters found that they could not achieve more than 33% utilization because of breakdowns and troubleshooting issues. Since then the machines have become much more reliable; companies with planned maintenance schedules can achieve a 75% utilization rate.

The issues faced by traditional service providers when trying to sell the new services are discussed later in the book. When TV was first introduced programming was just like radio programming— someone sat in front of a microphone reading the news. Clearly this did not take advantage of the benefits of the new technology. The same thing occurs today when printers try to sell on-demand or digital printing the same way they sold traditional printing.

SUMMARY

On-demand and digital color printing are accomplished when you print directly from computer programs such as Microsoft Word,

QuarkXPress, or Adobe PageMaker. Printruns are generally short (less then 5,000 impressions). The time spent for makeready and time devoted to binding is significantly reduced, resulting in reduced cycle times, lower costs, and the ability to perform shorter runs—resulting in a decreased chance of obsolescence. Market research organizations project continued growth of the short-run market, especially with the ability to better target retail customers with personalized and customized pieces.

There are disadvantages too. Although the time to print is faster, the quality is lower. Despite the fact that the reliability of the equipment has increased from 33% to 75%, the utilization rate in most companies remains between 25% and 50%. Although not as much of an issue for many in-plants, a utilization rate of 50% or less generally means that a commercial service provider is not breaking even. As a result, one of the greatest challenges for most commercial service providers is how to position and sell the products and services of these unique machines.

2 THE PRINTING PROCESSES

Printing may be defined as the reproduction of images affixed to a physically permanent substrate (as opposed to a television screen or computer monitor) in quantities of one or more. The act of printing requires an image carrier to transfer the image to a substrate, whether it be paper, foil, metal, glass, wood, or cloth. It is the nature of the image carrier that differentiates one printing process from another. Any two-dimensional image can be defined as having an image area and a nonimage area. These two distinct areas must be separated in some manner on an image carrier. Each of the printing principles described below varies in how the image and nonimage areas are kept distinct from one another.

The image areas of this lithographic printing plate appear in blue.

LITHOGRAPHY

The lithographic printing principle involves an image carrier with oil-attracting image areas and water-attracting nonimage areas. Because oil and water tend to repel each other, the image and nonimage areas on the image carrier are kept distinct from one another. The image carrier used in lithography is referred to as a plate which, when ready to be used for printing, is mounted on a printing press. The lithographic printing press is comprised of a series of rollers and cylinders. One set of rollers brings a water-based solution to the plate and another set brings an oil-based ink. The plate, which is wrapped around a cylinder, contacts the roller systems. The water clings to the nonimage areas of the plate while the oily ink sticks to the image areas of the plate. Then, the inked image is transferred to an intermediate cylinder (called the blanket cylinder). The inked image on the blanket cylinder is forced into contact with the paper by the pressure of the impression cylinder, thus transferring the image. So lithography is really a chemical printing process that is based upon the principle that ink and water repel each other.

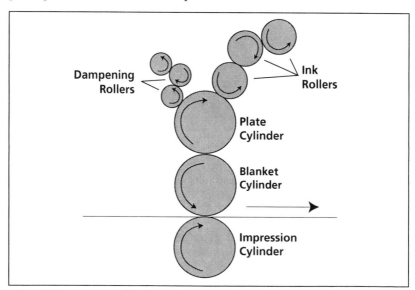

Ink and dampening rollers contact the plate in offset lithography.

LETTERPRESS

Letterpress printing is a relief process, meaning that the image is physically raised above a nonimage area. This is the principle referred to as relief printing. The image area comes into contact with an inked roller, and the nonimage area, being lower than the image area, does not get inked. An impression roller or platen forces that substrate against the relief image and thus an image is formed. Although some letterpress printing is done from flat type-forms, most modern letterpress printing uses curved or flexible plates mounted on a printing cylinder.

FLEXOGRAPHY

Flexography, a rapidly growing printing process used mainly in the packaging and newspaper printing segments of the graphic arts industry, is also a relief process, and is well suited for printing on foils and other types of nonabsorbent substrates. The process is called flexography because the image carrier, or flexographic plate, is made of a flexible rubber or polymer-based material. The process was introduced in the early 1900s as aniline printing, called this because of the type of inks used. But this name gave way to "flexography" in the late 1940s, the name of the process used exclusively today.

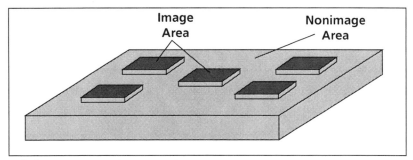

Relief image carriers have raised image areas.

GRAVURE

Gravure is an intaglio printing process. The image carrier has the image cut or etched below the surface of the nonimage area. On the gravure image carrier, all the images are screened creating thousands of tiny cells.

During printing, the image carrier is immersed in fluid ink. As the image carrier rotates, ink fills the tiny cells and covers the surface of the cylinder. The surface of the cylinder is wiped with a doctor blade leaving the nonimage area clean, while ink remains in the recessed cells. The substrate is brought into contact with the image carrier with the help of an impression roll. At the point of contact, ink is drawn out of the cells onto the substrate by capillary action.

Gravure is used for publications, catalogs, Sunday newspaper supplements, labels, folding cartons, flexible packaging, gift wrap, wall coverings, floor coverings, and a wide variety of coating applications.

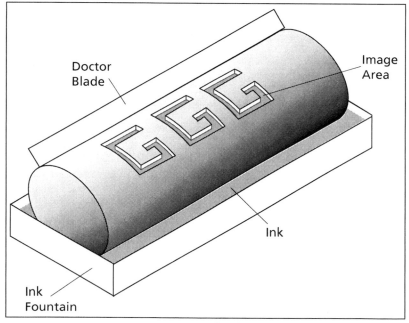

Rotogravure image carriers are engraved, either chemically or mechanically, so that the image areas are recessed.

SCREEN PRINTING

The screen printing process is used to print the widest variety of substrates of any printing process. In addition, many products for which screen printing is used can be printed by no other method. The principle of the process involves the use of a stencil that is adhered to a mesh material stretched on a frame. Ink is forced through the image areas of the mesh and onto a substrate with pressure exerted by a squeegee. This process is ideally suited for printing on rigid materials like metal and glass and is also used almost exclusively for printing on textiles. The process can also be used to print on cylindrical surfaces like ceramic mugs and plastic or glass bottles.

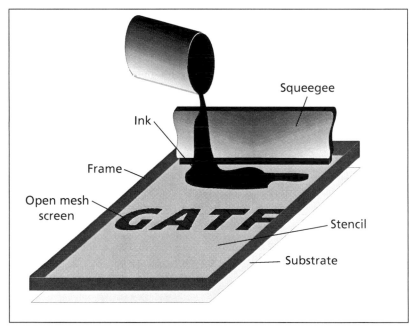

The screen printing process pushes ink through a fine screen, with nonimage areas blocked out by a stencil.

ELECTRONIC METHODS

Over the past several years, many electronic methods of printing have emerged. The oldest of these is the xerographic method, invented by Chester F. Carlson in the late 1930s. The printing process works by producing a positive electric charge on image areas of a selenium drum, while the nonimage areas of the drum have a negative or neutral charge. The drum is rotated over negatively-charged toner particles, which are attracted to the positive charge (image area) of the drum. The toner on the drum is then fused by heat to the paper. This printing principle is employed in much of today's low-volume printing equipment, most notably photocopy machines and laser printers. Other major electronic printing methods include ink-jet, thermal wax, and dye sublimation, each of which works on very different principles.

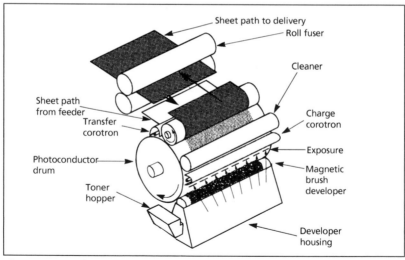

The principle of electrophotography.

3 WHAT IS ON-DEMAND PRINTING?

Whenever I speak to an audience about on-demand, digital, or custom printing, an argument always ensues over what exactly I am talking about. There is no consensus for the definitions of on-demand printing, on-demand presses, digital printing, and digital presses. They sound the same, but they are not.

DEFINING "ON-DEMAND"

The concept of on-demand is basically one of short notice and quick turnaround. For a movie or fax on demand service, one simply pushes a button or makes a phone call—on short notice one gets quick turnaround. In the printing industry, on-demand is also associated with shorter and usually more economical printing runs especially when comparing the price per unit for short run lengths. My definition of on-demand becomes "short notice, quick turnaround of short, economical print runs." When all criteria are met, they result in lower inventory costs, lower risk of obsolescence, lower production costs, and reduced distribution costs.

Most traditional printing does not fulfill these criteria and does not result in these advantages. The disadvantage of traditional long-run printing is that the reproduced information can become out-of-date, which requires the disposal of old material and re-manufacture of new material. In the United States, it is estimated that 31% of all traditional printing is discarded because it becomes obsolete.

Magazine publishing is a good example of this. Approximately one-third of all magazines displayed on a newsstand today are discarded. Many books are never sold, and some are even discarded by the bookseller. Another good example is the disposal of obsolete forms by forms manufacturers—tractor trailers filled with forms or data/specifications sheets that go to a landfill or dump because of product changes. The relentless push of technology causes products to be changed more frequently.

Notice that although most traditional printing does not fulfill this criteria, I do not associate any particular technology with the concept of on-demand. If one is clever or efficient or high-tech enough, one can produce on-demand printing with a traditional press.

For our intents and purposes, an on-demand press is any device that can print short runs, on short notice, relatively quickly, in a cost-efficient manner. This can be accomplished with a traditional press, a high-speed copier, a hybrid technology press, a high-quality printer, or a color copier. Lastly, the terms "on-demand printing" and "demand printing" will be used interchangeably.

DEFINING DIGITAL PRINTING

The definition of digital printing is a bit more difficult. A simple definition, and the one that I will use throughout the book, is that digital printing is any printing completed via digital files. Demand printing is economical, fast, and oriented to short runs while digital printing is printing from digital files, but is not restricted to short runs. Demand printing can be done with digital files or conventional film or plates, while digital printing is done only with digital files. My goal in this book is to cover all aspects of demand printing, with an emphasis on the digital presses that use new technology. Nevertheless I try to cover a larger area—namely, demand printing with any reproduction system.

DEFINING VARIABLE PRINTING

Traditional printing does not allow printing of variable information. With traditional printing, the prepress work is performed, the plates are made, and they are run on the press. The end result is thousands of pages that look exactly the same. This information is static and, therefore, not variable.

In contrast many of the digital presses (presses that print from digital data) can print variable information. Different names and addresses on different pages are possible. The ability to print variable information, which results in variable printing is the critical component of customized printing.

To accomplish customized printing today with the traditional printing technology described in Chapter 2 (i.e., lithography, flexography, etc.) conventional pages or static pages are run through high-speed inkjet devices for the variable information. This is how Publishers Clearinghouse Sweepstakes sends individuals a package that says, "Congratulations 'your name.' You have been picked as one of our finalists."

Although traditionally accomplished with high-speed inkjet devices, many of the digital presses offer this ability using their own electrophotographic or "copier-based" technology. An added advantage is that these devices are not limited to six or twelve lines of copy, as many of the inkjet devices are; some can customize the entire page. This is one of the most exciting elements of these devices.

These abilities allow variation of the contents of any single document or group of documents during a run. For instance, a cataloger could print 5,000 catalogs in lots of 500, each with a different cover. This could be used to test-market different covers. This is almost impossible and very cost prohibitive with traditional techniques.

There are as many ways to use variable information as the imagination will allow. The cataloger could include the recipient's name on each of the 1,000 direct mailers and vary a special insert based on demographics. The cataloger could also personalize sweatshirts and offer "iron-on" names.

The building blocks of customized printing are the combination of variable information with output devices that do not require intermediate films or plates. They are true digital printing systems in that all or part of the image area can be changed from impression to impression.

If one considers the amount of mailings received where one's name is built into the message, one senses the tremendous market for personalization and customization of text and images. The objective of any direct mail piece is to encourage one to read it and entice one to buy it! Personalization accomplishes this because one is more apt to read something that grabs one's interest.

MY DEFINITION

My definition of a printing process capable of variable printing is one that can incorporate data from a database and does not use non-digital technologies such as film or plates. How does the definition of variable printing interact with previous definitions? Completely independently. A demand press may or may not be able to print variable pages, and a digital press may or may not be able to print variable pages.

WHAT ARE TYPICAL RUN LENGTHS?

The best definition of a short run is one that is less than 5,000 impressions. How much work is done at this run length? Almost 56% of commercial, book, and office printing (including duplicating and copying) falls in the category of run lengths from 500 to 5,000 impressions.

It is interesting that only 2.8% of this printing is done in four or more colors. But, these numbers represent the trends today. According to the market research discussed later, by the year 2000 the amount of four-color printing in this run-length market will more than quadruple to 11.5%. In fact, color will increase as a percentage of total reproduced pages as it becomes easier to accomplish on new and traditional equipment.

Traditional printing presses generally operate in the long-run category and above. Recently, however, many printers have been attempting to compete with moderate or even short-run categories to remain competitive. Technological advances that can be applied

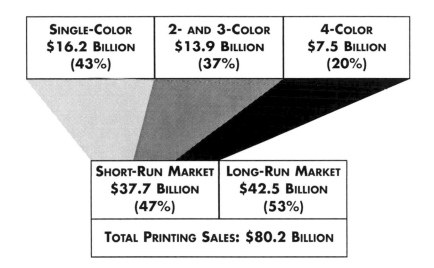

SINGLE-COLOR $16.2 BILLION (43%)	2- AND 3-COLOR $13.9 BILLION (37%)	4-COLOR $7.5 BILLION (20%)

SHORT-RUN MARKET $37.7 BILLION (47%)	LONG-RUN MARKET $42.5 BILLION (53%)
TOTAL PRINTING SALES: $80.2 BILLION	

CAPV projections for the on-demand market.

to traditional presses, such as quick-change plate capability, on-press densitometry, calibrated adjustments, and waterless offset, could move some presses into the short-run category routinely. That is why we have left the definition of demand printing open to any technology. It is possible for clever printers to accomplish on-demand printing with traditional presses.

Most traditional presses as we know them now, however, will have difficulty in meeting the needs of the short-run category and below. This is where a new market is developing. Based on market projections and my conversations with printers, I project that the short-run wars will take place in the 100- to 3,000-run length range. Above that, newer printing presses will be competitive, and below that, newer plain-paper color printers will evolve.

SHORT-RUN PROCESS COLOR PRINTING

Run lengths from 100 to 1,500 are ideal for digital color presses. Beyond that it is difficult to turn a profit. Digital printing allows a printer to serve its customers by storing multiple-page documents that are needed in small quantities, on-demand. It also allows a printer to offer full variable color printing in which every document can be different or have a personal message.

ON-DEMAND PRINTING AND PUBLISHING CONCEPTS

In an oversimplification of the on-demand process, the client supplies electronic files or camera-ready materials and specifies how many copies of the publication will be needed. The printer produces the publication directly from the disk or camera-ready artwork and delivers it within a specified timeframe.

There are many aspects to the process that make it more than simple. With short-run work, it is necessary to automate the job submission so that all information about the job accompanies the actual electronic file. This is only one aspect of on-demand that escapes potential users. Short runs imply that more jobs will be passing through a facility, with average runs of under 1,000. This will force the modification of order entry, estimating, scheduling, customer service, and billing procedures.

Currently there are three specific on-demand strategies in our industry: on-demand printing, distributed demand printing, and on-demand publishing. Except for rare occasions when traditionally prepared and printed short runs are fast and economical, most of the time the expression "on-demand" means that the data is stored and printed in electronic form. It doesn't have to be an electronic file, but generally it is a digital file that facilitates the efficacy of the short run.

The second strategy is known as distributed demand printing. Unlike the general concept of demand printing, the distributed demand printing workflow requires that the electronic files can be transmitted to other locations via phone lines or satellite transmission, printed, and distributed locally. These publications can then be stored, printed, and shipped locally as needed. This is an implementation of the distribute-and-print philosophy as opposed to the traditional print-and-distribute philosophy.

The traditional long-run printing strategy is to print large volumes in a central location and then ship them both long (nationally) and short distances (regionally). Decentralization does reduce shipping costs but does not eliminate storage and distribution costs. Combining on-demand printing with decentralization produces the best results.

The third general strategy is demand publishing in which the data is stored in paginated form and transmitted for immediate printout. Large-volume magazines do this, which allows them to provide regional inserts. Portable Document Formats, such as Adobe Acrobat or No Hands Common Ground, are being used to distribute the paginated and print-ready page and document files.

Another example of this is fax publishing, which makes every fax machine a printing press. Paginated and formatted files are transmitted for printout. Quality is still an issue, but over time any printer may be fax-like and resolutions of 600 dpi or more would be possible.

THE FUTURE OF ON-DEMAND

In the future, this definition of on-demand printing may change to include binding or finishing. Ultimately, on-demand printing requires both an imaging engine and a means of combining in consecutive, uninterrupted operations the printed pages into finished products— college textbooks, out-of-print books, insurance policies, research reports, business proposals, or any other reproduced products.

Printing with in-line finishing puts very stringent demands on the condition and reliability of the equipment used. When any part of the line is down, the whole system is down. Also, printing and finishing require different skills and operators will require both kinds.

As I will discuss in the next chapter, two significant advantages of on-demand printing are the decreased time to get the first acceptable page printed (makeready) and the ability to print a finished product (binding).

4 Economics of On-Demand

There has always been a demand for shorter printing runs, but various hurdles impeded the successful delivery of this service. The traditional methods of creating printed pieces are more expensive because of the associated prepress, press, and postpress costs. Prepress costs include the hardware (computers) and software (page-layout programs) as well as price of the scanners, output devices, film, processing chemistry, and plates. Press costs include makeready (preparation) costs, and, usually, long printing runs due to price breaks for longer runs. Postpress costs include the time and cost of collating, binding, and finishing.

These costs are significantly lower in on-demand printing due to shorter makeready time, lack of prepress work, and in-line binding and finishing.

Some of these steps remain important regardless of printing technology, such as the coordination of design, typesetting, and page layout. Some steps are associated with traditional offset printing such as photography, additional film work, stripping, manual imposition, proofing, platemaking, and press startup, but are later consolidated with improved workflows. The desktop workflow, for example, usually uses scanning instead of photography, electronic imposition instead of manual imposition, elimination of stripping by using imposition programs, PostScript, and imagesetters and/or platesetters.

THE ECONOMICS OF LONG RUNS

Traditional printing costs become more cost-effective, in terms of per-unit costs, as run lengths increase. In contrast, electrophotographic or photocopying technologies have fixed costs that remain the same regardless of run length. Copying usually does not require additional film work, stripping, manual imposition, proofing, platemaking, or press startup. These factors, combined with the low cost of the equipment and toner, allow copying to be cost-effective for very short runs.

As a result, copying results in fixed costs that do not change as run length increases. In contrast, offset, and other forms of printing, result in variable costs. Thus, the per-unit cost of copying does not change as the run length changes, but the per-unit cost of printing is reduced as run length increases.

New technologies, such as computer-to-plate and automated presses, are applying techniques that allow a press to perform makeready in record time and are thus able to produce shorter runs. On-demand concepts, therefore, do not exclude the use of traditional printing presses.

On-demand printing, utilizing electrophotographic techniques, is clearly advantageous up to 1,000 pages. In the range from 1,000 to 6,000, however, there is overlap, and the technology that is less expensive depends on the specific job.

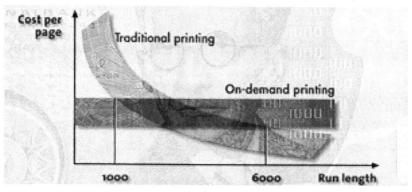

Courtesy of Agfa, a division of Bayer USA

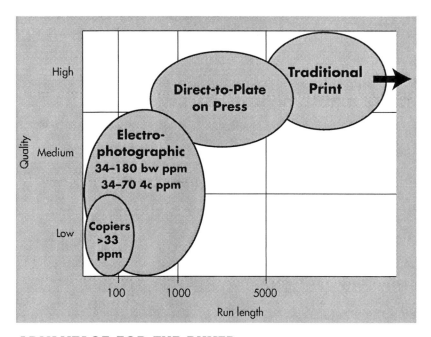

ADVANTAGE FOR THE BUYER

The benefits of demand printing for print buyers are substantial—it allows companies to introduce products to the market faster, make last-minute revisions, and reduce or eliminate costly warehousing. And, digital printing allows for the creation of personalized and custom-printed products for use in targeted marketing campaigns.

THE EFFICIENCIES OF DIGITAL AND ON-DEMAND WORKFLOWS

The time and cost to manufacture a printed product using a digital workflow is typically less than creating the same piece using a conventional workflow. Here's an example of the workflow, time, and costs to prepare and print a page in color at a quantity of 500. Since there are so many possible workflows, this is merely an example:

1. **Creative development.** The creative area has been most affected by desktop technology. Most art and design professionals now create their pages with desktop computers. It is

the by-product of this process that results in electronic pages. These costs should not be calculated in the final cost of the reproduction of the job.

I repeat—none of the costs associated with the creative process are calculated in the cost of reproducing pages. For some, this is an issue. If a financially trained person calculated a return on investment (ROI) equation for a purchase, he or she would calculate the equipment, personnel, and overhead. Another way to think about this is that, in the traditional workflow, the creative personnel acquired type and art from commercial services and were charged. Those charges exist no matter how the job is reproduced.

2. **Film output.** Most production work today is done by the designer. He or she creates the pages, proofs them on low-cost laser printers, and sends them to a service bureau for printout on photographic paper or film. Costs vary significantly, but most printouts are at about $7 per page for photo paper and $19 for film (black and white). A set of four films with a film-based proof for four-color printing would probably sell for about $60.

3. **Separations and proofing.** Just as the price of output varies, the price of scanning and proofing vary as well. A further complicating factor is that alternative image acquisition options are continuously eating away at the amount of work done on high-end scanners. Therefore, digital photography, PhotoCDs, and desktop scanners will be used more and more regardless of the workflow or printing technology. For this example however, the cost is $60.

4. **Stripping.** Just as typographers have become extinct, so too will strippers. (Sorry, it's not our fault.) Traditionally, strippers would inspect the film for quality and pinholes, opaque the pinholes with a special brush and liquid so that light would not pass through, strip the page units onto a special sheet, and finally inspect for alignment and quality. Once again, consumables (the special sheet), labor, and equipment

are the cost areas. Printing industry cost standards are presently about $60 per hour, or about $35 per page. For our purposes, the cost is approximately $70 per page.

5. **Platemaking.** Platemaking, the final step in the prepress process, is varied for different types of printing. For the sake of simplicity, let's say that a printer uses a photographic process to expose the reversed image from the negative film separation onto a flat metal or paper plate. At this point, the image on the plate is right-reading (you can read it). It has a chemical coating that attracts ink but not water while the nonimage area attracts water but repels ink. Platemaking typically costs about $70.

6. **Makeready/printing.** Makeready is essentially all the work done to set up a printing press to deliver the first acceptable page. For this example, let's say that it takes one hour for both the makeready and printing at $100.

7. **Paper.** Paper costs have been escalating, and paper is also becoming more difficult to get. The cost of paper includes the required stock, including any waste for makeready. For this job, we'll say we used some leftover paper that the printer wanted to get rid of that was $15. (Once again, paper costs are highly variable, and should be calculated in a comparison of machine costs.)

To summarize traditional reproduction:

	Per page	Hours
Film output	$60	1.0
Color separations	$60	0.5
Stripping	$70	1.0
Platemaking	$70	0.5
Makeready/printing	$100	1.0
Paper	$15	–
Total	$375	4.0

These costs may vary from printer to printer, and region to region, but major industry associations publish cost standards so that all printers can measure their productivity and cost-effectiveness.

As in the following example, the cost of conventional color reproduction carries high prepress and preparatory costs. This immediately negates the ability to produce short runs cost-effectively.

Alternative workflows utilizing desktop and electronic systems are attempting to bypass some of those steps. One of the advantages of the PostScript workflow is that you print four pieces of final film from a PostScript imagesetter, eliminating costs associated with stripping and platemaking.

	Per page	Hours
Film output (RIP time)	$20	0.5
Color separations	$40	0.5
Stripping	–	–
Platemaking	–	–
Printing	$200	0.5
Paper	$10	–
Total	$270	1.5

In this example, on-demand reduces the cost of printing by 28%, and the time by 62.5%. We believe that using a digital press workflow offers a similar set of savings to the desktop workflow, as the desktop workflow provides for the conventional workflow. If we used a digital press, several steps would be eliminated. With digital printing there is no stripping, platemaking, or makeready. As a result, digital printing can result in a savings of about 30% in dollars and 60% in time.

5 COMPETING WITH COPIERS

Today most of the on-demand products use electrophotographic or copier-based technology. The question becomes "Will this technology continue to dominate the on-demand market?" New black-and-white and color copiers are incorporating the laser printer technology that will allow them to compete as on-demand systems.

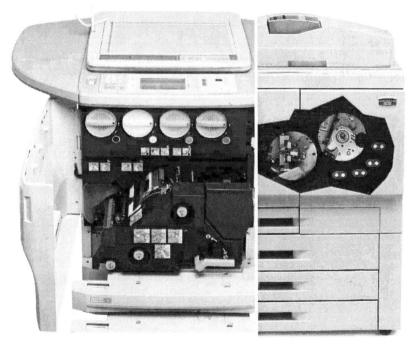

Inside a color copier.

Other technologies can fulfill the same requirements. Sometimes they are in direct competition with electrophotography, sometimes they offer totally distinct features that mark them for different applications. Among the characteristics on which competitive technologies can be compared are speed, hardware cost, cost per copy, ability to do continuous-tone printing, image permanence, and media restrictions.

The three technologies that have the greatest chance of competing are electrostatic, inkjet, and thermal transfer. As you will see in the more in-depth description that follows, the toughest technology to differentiate from electrophotographic is electrostatic, because electrophotographic printing uses electrostatic principles. The differences are in the formation of the charge image and the need for special paper.

Inkjet and thermal transfer are easier to distinguish. Inkjet works by spraying one or more colors of ink that are aimed by electric field deflectors (electromagnetically) onto paper. It can favorably compete on a cost-per-image basis and on page-per-minute rates. Permanence of the color image remains a question with water-based inks, and quality is an important issue.

Thermal printers apply heat to a ribbon carrying waxed ink to transfer it to paper. All variants of thermal transfer printing do not offer the printing speed for high-end printing and copying applications. The highest-quality thermal transfer is dye diffusion, due to its continuous nature. However, it is also the most expensive on a unit-image basis.

ELECTROSTATIC (ELECTROGRAPHIC) TECHNOLOGY

Equivalent to electrophotography in many respects, electrostatic technology (electrography or dielectric) differs in the method of forming the electrostatic image. Recall that electrophotography discharges, via light, a photoconductor that has been "sprayed" with an electric charge.

Electrography, on the other hand, places a charge on specially coated paper where an image, or dot, is to be formed. A wire "nib" print head, comes in contact with the dielectric coated paper at a suitable voltage, and places a charge on the paper. Four passes of the print head are required to create a full-color image.

In most configurations, the charged image on the paper is toned and then the paper is rewound, and the next image charged (representing the next color) is placed on the paper. This process is repeated until all four colors are printed. The development of the electrostatic image is identical to electrophotography. However, liquid development is the method of choice due to simplicity and cost for wide formats.

Dry toner development would be more difficult and costly over such large widths due to the increased complexities of the magnetic brush development system. Like electrophotography, electrography yields images of high permanence and resistance to light, water, and mechanical abrasion. These images contain toner that has a lower fraction of polymer (plastic) than electrophotography, so the images do not have a plastic-coated look and feel.

INKJET

Inkjet printing can be divided into two basic categories: continuous and drop-on-demand (DOD). Continuous inkjet, which had its beginnings in the early 1960s in the recording of electrical signals on a paper chart, employs a continuous stream of fluid. Natural forces cause the continuous stream to randomly break up into little droplets.

The process parallels that of a garden hose: the water first comes out as a stream, but before it hits the ground, drops of various sizes are formed. This random breakup is totally unsatisfactory for printing since the drops can not be placed accurately on the paper surface. A solution to this problem is to "stimulate" breakup by applying a high-frequency pressure variation to the ink stream, causing the drops to form in a known and repeatable manner.

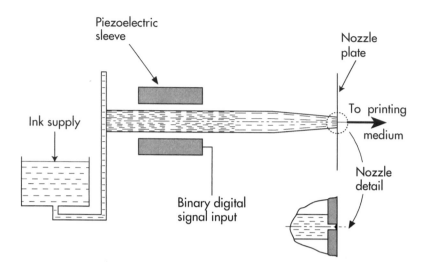

Drop-on-demand inkjet technology.   Courtesy of Wolfgang Wehl, Siemens AG, and reprinted by permission of SPSE: The Society for Imaging Science and Technology.

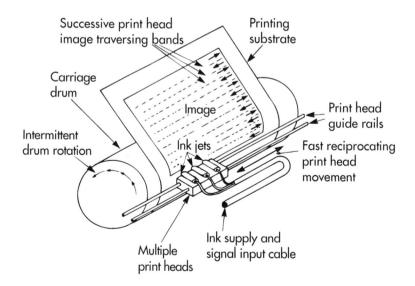

An inkjet positioning and paper feed mechanism.

By putting an electrical charge on the drop, at the instant it breaks from the continuous stream, and letting the charged drop fly through an electrical field, the position of the drop on the paper can be precisely controlled. Drops that are not directed or written to the paper are deflected to an ink recirculating system to be used again. An advantage to be gained from using the continuous inkjet method is that the fluid is not afforded the opportunity to dry in the nozzles.

The drop-on-demand (DOD) inkjet method has been described as the "oil can." A closed chamber with a small nozzle at one end, and filled with ink, is reduced in volume via a piezoelectric actuator. The decrease in chamber volume forces the ink fluid out through the nozzle.

A variation on this theme is thermal inkjet, or "bubble jet," in which, instead of reducing the ink chamber volume, the fluid ink is expanded by heating a small volume of ink, forcing a drop out the nozzle. The drop ejection rates of the inkjet printers are limited to perhaps 20,000 drops/second largely due to the complexities of refilling the ink chamber. Increasing the printing speed of DOD inkjet technology would require a multiple-nozzle or array approach.

Most inkjet products, whether continuous or drop-on-demand, use water as the ink fluid to carry the colorant. The water can evaporate at various times and cause nozzle clogging, which plagued early inkjet products. Water, as the fluid base, poses additional challenges when it interacts with paper. Ink bleeding within the paper causes the spot to grow, sometimes in an irregular manner, resulting in poor print quality. For color, the ink/paper interaction problems are accentuated because color formation demands that ink drops be placed on top of each other. This increases the amount of ink that must be absorbed by the paper.

An additional consideration for color printing is the colorant (dye) in the ink. It must reside on the top of the paper in order to produce saturated colors. To achieve this, several vendors have developed special inkjet paper. These factors are the primary reasons why inkjet is not considered a plain-paper process.

One very distinct advantage of the liquid ink products is their ability to make very high-quality color transparencies. The high quality is a result of using dyes as the colorants, instead of pigment particles that are used in thermal transfer. Pigment particles scatter light, and in a projected transparency this results in an image that is dark and much less colorful than its paper counterpart.

Permanence of images is an important issue facing inkjet technology. When speaking of permanence we generally mean:

- Resistance of image smearing when water is applied
- The ability to retain colors after exposure to light
- Image resistance to mechanical factors

Color images made from water-based inks usually are very susceptible to water spilled on them. Most inkjet inks use dyes as the colorant material—and dyes are known to fade. A crucial question is how long will the images retain their original color. Some inkjet systems have exhibited fading under office lighting within months, while others show only small color changes over a period of years. Careful formulation of water-based inks is leading to increased permanence for inkjet images.

Jet clogging, which necessitated complex and costly print head maintenance stations, has for the most part disappeared in newer products. For the long run, inkjet is probably the strongest competitor to electrophotography for high-volume printing—largely because of its low print cost. Large print volumes will bring the cost of the special paper down, and inks are basically inexpensive.

THERMAL TRANSFER

A color printing technology that has seen significant growth, in terms of units sold, is thermal transfer printing. Thermal printing has a varied history, but the technology has gravitated into two forms, categorized in terms of their imaging materials:

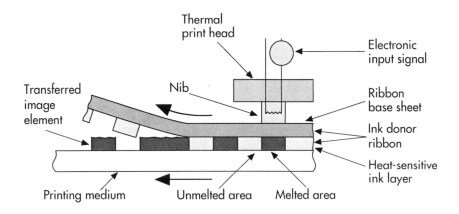

Thermal transfer printing. Courtesy of *Journal of Applied Photographic Engineering*, vol 7, 1981 by SPSE

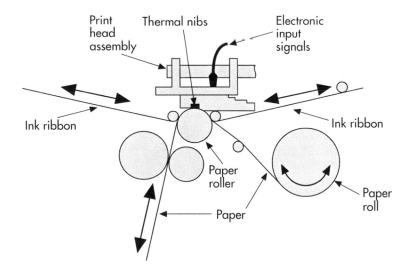

Thermal transfer print engine. Courtesy of Seiko Instruments, Inc.

- Thermal wax transfer, in which the imaging material is a pigmented "wax"
- Thermal dye transfer, in which colored dyes comprise the imaging material

The basic components of a thermal transfer device are:
- A thermal print head comprised of a series of small heating elements spaced at 200 to 300 per inch
- Ink/dye donor sheet, the source of the image colorant
- Paper or receiver sheet
- A pressure roll

Applying an electrical current to the resistive heating element in the thermal print head causes it to become hot. The thermal head is in intimate contact with the donor sheet—assured by a pressure roll or platen opposite to the print head. As the imaging material heats up (about 100°C), it melts the wax. In the case of thermal dye transfer, the heat (300°C) drives a dye into the paper.
- Thermal wax transfer is bilevel in that only two levels can be produced; ink is transferred or no ink is transferred to the paper.
- For thermal dye transfer, a continuum of dye can be transported to the receiver or paper according to the amount of heat energy applied.

Image and print size for both methods are limited by print head size and the mechanics that move the ink donor web and paper. An 11-in. head seems to be about the maximum size available, although larger heads are possible. Neither of these thermal transfer techniques can be considered "plain paper."

THERMAL WAX
Thermal wax transfer is somewhat more costly than inkjet. The higher-quality thermal dye transfer, with its specially coated paper and multi-layer dye donor web, is significantly more expensive.

Thermal transfer has low imaging material utilization. Only 30% to 60% of each of the colorant layers is transferred—the remainder is thrown away.

THERMAL DYE

Thermal dye transfer is a continuous process. Because of its ability to transfer different amounts of colorant, according to the total heat energy applied, it does not require halftoning techniques. In fact if the number of levels is sufficient, say about 32 or more, a 200-dpi image can pass for "photographic quality."

Thermal dye transfer is also called "dye diffusion" and "dye sublimation" in attempts to explain the actual process of migrating dye molecules from donor to receiver sheet. Thermal dye transfer technology shows promise in several emerging color applications, including video/electronic camera output, prepress proofing, and medical imaging.

However, in addition to far higher supplies costs, there are considerable performance costs: an "A" size print takes up to 3 minutes to complete. The plain paper/higher speed vs. superior print quality issues may lead to interesting market battles in the few areas of application overlap between inkjet and thermal dye transfer.

SUMMARY

As a technology, electrophotography has the advantage in the high-volume color copying and printing areas. Two factors account for this: low unit-image cost and high process speed. It is unlikely that any of the existing color technologies will become competitive on these factors in the near future. As a consequence of high hardware costs, color electrophotographic technology will not migrate to lower volume/speed ranges in the near term.

The color hardcopy market has emerged much more slowly than many observers originally expected, plagued by the early reliability problems, high costs, and the lack of a clear user mandate for graphic applications. Recently, acceptance of color has accelerated. Electrophotography will play a dual role in the development of the overall color market. Color copiers will promote use of all output technologies by facilitating the production of multiple copies for distribution. Color printers will offer plain-paper output at unprecedented speeds, making a scenario of color-based on-demand publishing realistic.

In the printing and publishing segment, the strongest position for color electrophotography will be for on-demand publishing, which is expected to grow as an extension of desktop publishing.

The color electrophotographic copiers and printers that are coming to market are part of an evolutionary process that dates back fifty years. Electrophotography has many significant advantages over competitive technologies: excellent output quality, high imaging and process speeds, low cost per page, and plain-paper capability. These attributes have extended monochrome electrophotographic configurations into many operating environments, with products ranging from less-than-$1,000 personal copiers to 200+ page-per-minute laser printers. Developers of color systems hope to use the same attributes to gain a strong position in the color hardcopy arena, although the complexity of color may limit the product range.

Color electrophotography's development and market positioning is characterized by several factors:

- High research-and-development costs have limited participation to a few major imaging companies, such as Canon, Fuji, Xerox, and Japanese companies.
- Although price/performance gains have been made with each new generation of product, color electrophotography has a starting level of close to $20,000, which has restricted its market presence.

Monochrome electrophotography made its mark in the copier area, expanding into printing applications as reliability improved and software was developed that took advantage of the technology's strengths. A similar migration from copier to printer configurations happened with color electrophotography.

6 THE ROLE OF PAPER

Riddle:
What factor slowed the availability of printed products immediately after the invention of the first printing press as well as after the digital presses shipped?

Answer: The availability and cost of paper.

CIRCA 300 YEARS AGO

For 300 years after the invention of Gutenberg's press, most publications were out of the reach of the average European. The problem was not press technology but rather the high cost of paper, which, until the end of the 18th century, was made by hand from the pulp of linen rags. It wasn't until the 1790s that a clerk named Nicholas-Louis Robert recognized that there was a future in cheaper paper and left his position in a Paris publishing house to learn the art of papermaking.

Several obstacles stood in his path. He had to leave the papermill at the great paper center of Essonnes because he didn't get along with the employees. But he persisted and created a prototype machine, though it wasn't commercially acceptable. Bryan Donkin, an English engineer, took Robert's idea and turned it into the first practical papermaking machine. Ultimately the papermaking machine took off throughout Europe, Russia, and America, and the 19th century was being called the "Age of Paper."

CIRCA THREE YEARS AGO

After the introduction of some electrostatic presses, an erasability problem was discovered. A special paper treatment was subsequently developed. At first, treated paper was only available in limited quantity and on limited stocks. Some companies frustrated by the limited availability bought the pretreatment machine themselves.

After the early machines were delivered, only a limited number of suitable paper stocks were available. Many of the paper stocks are made in Europe and manufactured for the European-designed press. Some U.S.-based users had to buy these huge rolls of paper and get them shipped to the United States. This was not a good solution.

Shipping the rolls was expensive, and the delivery times were long. When they did arrive, they had to be rerolled to fit on a common U.S. roll size. These factors fly in direct conflict with the selling points of on-demand printing: fast turnaround and low cost.

The issues for the paper for on-demand presses center on availability, runnability, price, and delivery time. Is the paper available locally, nationally, or internationally, and how long will it take to get it? Will the paper run untreated or does it need a pretreatment? Will the high temperature of the fuser cause inconsistent toner adhesion or make the paper discolor or blister? Can it be bought in small lots or large rolls? Are there added costs for pretreatment or size conversion?

The moral of the story is that printing technology alone is not enough. Successful printing also requires the availability of low-cost paper.

ELECTROPHOTOGRAPHIC PAPERS

Despite the dreams of the paperless office in the 1980s and the infatuation with the Internet today, the fact remains that paper is the overwhelming tool of choice for business communication. It may be copy machines, laser printers, or fax machines—all of these office machines are available as electrophotographic devices.

Paper quality influences the quality and productivity of electro-photographic printing. In paper terms, this is known as the print-ability or the quality of the image as printed, and runnability or how well the paper performs in the printing or copying process.

Choosing the right paper for those devices is critical. The right paper ensures accuracy, reliability, and permanence. The right paper is designed to meet manufacturer's standards for printability, readability, toner retention, moisture content, and strength. And lastly, the right paper should not jam or misfeed. Here are a few criteria to consider before choosing a paper for electrophotographic engines.

WEIGHT

Weight affects a paper's durability and its ability to move through the print engine. Other important attributes that also help avoid jams are accurate trimming to proper size, proper surface characteristics, stiffness, and the ability to withstand intense heat.

Paper is often identified by its basis weight. Basis weight or sub-stance is the weight versus its surface area. For example, standard copy paper is known as "20 pound" or "sub(stance) 20" bond. Most popular papers are bought and sold at a number of dollars per ton, or per hundred weight, or per pound. The basis weight is the weight in pounds of one ream (500 sheets) cut to the grade's basic size.

Every paper grade has its own typical basic size. The basic size of bond paper is 17×22 in. A ream of 500 sheets of 20-lb. bond paper at its basic size weighs 20 lb. These reams will be cut into four 5-lb. reams of 8.5×11-in., 20-lb. bond paper used for office copiers. Similarly a ream of 24-lb. bond paper in its basic size weighs 24 lb.

TONER ADHERENCE

Toner adherence is a critical factor in electrophotographic-based printing. The three factors that determine toner adherence are:
- Paper curl
- Moisture content
- Electrical properties (conductivity and resistivity)

OTHER CRITERIA FOR CHOOSING A PAPER

Other factors that influence output include smoothness, opacity, brightness, long-term storage (archival) needs, and recycled content. For paper to accept toner best, it needs a level surface and a fine smooth finish. This is most obvious with flat tints of pictures (halftones) that contain fine screens or subtle tones. Opacity affects a document's legibility and is determined by the thickness of the paper. A paper with high opacity allows no "show-through" from the other side, which is required for two-sided imaging.

Similar to opacity, brightness affects readability as well as how well the images "pop" off the page. The brighter the paper, the more legible the type and the greater the contrast of the graphics.

For archival documents (documents that are stored for extended periods of time), special paper is required. These specially made acid-free papers can extend the document's life to 200 years or more.

7 COMMERCIAL APPLICATIONS

Commercial printers and quick printers serve a vital role. Committed to serving the diverse printing needs, they produce a wide variety of products. Historically, quick printers, or what today are referred to as "convenience" printers, have carved out a unique niche in the printing market based on fast turnaround. However, commercial printers under competitive pressure from convenience printers are being forced to provide faster turnarounds. The problem is that the batch-oriented nature of the commercial printing business makes it difficult to remain competitive.

Printing is a batch-oriented process. Large printing presses fed by sophisticated prepress systems produce long runs. Long runs are virtually mandated in order to absorb the traditional makeready costs of the process. It is not very different from an assembly line. Commercial printing, therefore, is a manufacturing process, and like other manufacturing processes, improvements can be made either with more efficient technology or through innovative management philosophies.

JUST IN TIME

Print production is a manufacturing process, and innovations to manufacturing processes, such as digital printing, benefit the entire processes. As a manufacturing process, print production could benefit from new management concepts such as "just in time" (JIT), SPC (statistical process control), and TQM (total quality management). The concept of "just-in-time" delivery of parts or supplies reduces inventories and eliminates waste for manufacturers, such as when a supplier delivers parts to the factory floor just in time for their incorporation into a product.

JIT has enabled many different manufacturers to dramatically reduce on-site storage of supplies or parts without loss. In fact, there are usually gains in productivity. Suppliers deliver goods in smaller quantities more frequently and dependably, and timed more closely to when they are needed.

Buyers of printing are seeking similar advantages. They want the ability to acquire only what they need—when they need it. This has already become evident in the book market where short-run book printing has grown significantly over the last decade. JIT philosophies are therefore affecting the purchasing of printed products.

I project that customers will demand shorter, more economical printing, faster and only when they need it. These advantages are possible with on-demand and digital color printing. Described below are the applications that are the best and worst fit for on-demand, digital, and customized printing.

APPROPRIATE APPLICATIONS FOR ON-DEMAND AND DIGITAL PRINTING

Although we could list 500 or more applications for these technologies, instead we have listed the more popular categories. In the terms of best-fit applications, we see the following: advertising/direct mail, author reprints, books/manuals, bound galleys, brochures/booklets, catalogs, envelope/packaging, financial/legal, flyer/folder, form/coupon, invitation/menu, letterhead/stationery, newspaper, and signs/posters.

ADVERTISING/DIRECT MAIL

Advertising and direct mail marketing are characterized by the heavy use of illustrations and color, with a wide variety of type styles and heavy use of graphics. Although different in their method of delivery, the goals are the same—to motivate people to buy products.

In contrast to advertisements that normally run in publications along side of editorial pages, direct mail is a stand-alone product delivered right to your mailbox. As we explain in the chapter on database marketing, direct mail can be easily customized.

On-demand digital color technology is being tested for sophisticated direct mail production. There will be an explosion of personalized promotions with personalization such as sales letters containing pictures of the sales person and the product. But could national advertising become customized?

The way we work today, the answer is "no." Today advertisements are still provided to newspapers and magazines as film or hard copy.

For the first time in almost a decade, standards committees have developed a standard for advertisement transmission called TIFF-IT. The TIFF-IT or ANSI IT 8.8 standard contains the three main components of a digital standard—image content, linework description, and high-resolution continuous-tone information content.

One of the advantages of TIFF-IT is that it allows advertisers, trade shops, publishers, and printers to continue to use their existing equipment and methods at the desktop publishing level, as well as the traditional high-end CEPS (color electronic prepress systems; e.g., Linotype-Hell, Scitex, DuPont Crosfield). This new standard will bring publications into the realm of digital printing since all parts of the publication would then be in electronic form. Digital advertising is essential for digital printing.

Once there are TIFF-IT readers and writers, publishers or printers could open up a standard advertisement and possibly customize it for certain areas or demographics.

AUTHOR REPRINTS

The author of a journal article is usually entitled to 100 or so extra copies of the article to circulate to colleagues. Typically, these reprints are produced by cutting apart extra copies of the printed journal—a labor-intensive undertaking, and one that usually happens weeks after the print run.

With electronic printing, the author's copies can be created from the same PostScript files used to create the journal, and can be printed while the journal is still on the press.

BOOKS/MANUALS

Books, characterized by high page counts, are typically black-and-white documents with a relatively consistent text format. Although black-and-white is the most popular format for books, the use of color is projected to increase. Books are one of the most appropriate applications for these technologies.

Also included in this category are manuals, technical documentation, proposals, and reports, which are the most popular electronic publishing applications. Directories are included here, with small overlap with catalogs.

One aspect of production that contributes to the cost of products in this category is collating and binding. Binding is usually adhesive (perfect binding) or sewn, although mechanical binding is also used. The dream of on-demand digital printing is that it will produce books on-demand. This may not be so much a printing problem as a binding problem.

BOUND GALLEYS

Initial reviews of a book are generally written before the book itself is printed. They are based on "bound galleys," which represent an intermediate stage when the content is complete, but final editing and page makeup have not occurred. Using traditional printing techniques, creating bound galleys for reviewers is extremely expensive. Although expensive, it is a necessary step if the reviews are to be published before the book hits the stores. With on-demand and digital printing, bound galleys can be created readily from an electronic manuscript at any stage.

BROCHURES/BOOKLETS

Typically, brochures and booklets are produced from multiple-folded paper (less than 100 pages) grouped into sets and stapled through the fold (saddle stitched). We predict that products in this category are expected to increase in color usage as a result of the new technologies.

As described in the in-plant chapter, these documents are important for large companies. They are used both in internal and external communications. Also, online bindery functions will allow new electronic printers to produce completed brochures, which would increase the number of products in this category.

CATALOGS

Specialized catalogs lend themselves well to the advantages of on-demand printing and publishing, especially when combined with variable information. With electronic printing, it is possible to customize different versions.

As a result, you could select certain items appropriate for a specific region (i.e., winter coats for northern regions), a specific trade show (i.e., the Graph Expo printing show), or a specific customer type and publish a custom-tailored catalog. With the advent of high-speed, on-demand, digital printing, this type of catalog marketing will increase.

Although not as well-known, another type of catalog is the industrial catalog, which is essentially groups of product sheets. These are appropriate for digital printing using variable information.

Other products that could be included in this category are flyers, brochures, or booklets used for marketing and contain considerable process-color pages. We project that more single-sheet and four-page units will be utilized once competitive costs are available.

FORMS/COUPONS

Fill-in forms are characterized by high usage of horizontal and vertical rules. It is difficult to generalize about the content because the formats are very erratic, except for the fact that they contain lines of text and a place for a signature.

Essentially, a form contains some amount of canned or repetitive data combined with variable or personalized data. This is a perfect application for digital printing since it has the long-term ability to change the page image on each page, where traditional printing repeats the same image on every page.

MAGAZINE REPRINTS

Magazine reprints are an excellent application for digital and on-demand technology. Often, when a company orders reprints, they are used as sales tools. Since there is often an unprinted area or white space on the reprint, it is well suited for customized printing.

Another advantage is that the magazine reprints can be ready when the article hits the newsstand. Today, it may take weeks or months to receive reprints. Often the publisher, printer, or fulfillment company waits until there is enough pent-up demand to justify a print run. With digital and on-demand technology, reprints can be made faster, for less money, and customized for specific purposes such as sales.

NEWSPAPERS

While the benefits of this technology to most other applications are fairly obvious, this category often surprises people. That is because newspapers are large-circulation publications and large in format size. Categorized as either broadsheet or tabloid (half a broadsheet), they are printed and folded in one pass through the printing press, often containing several sections and inserts. When it comes to news delivery, however, newspapers that are quick to adopt alternative delivery will not only survive, but thrive. This alternative delivery could be online service, fax publishing, or on-demand printing.

Some newspapers use fax delivery. Currently, the *New York Times* and *London Times* produce a fax newspaper that is sent to certain hotels, cruise ships, and resorts. The fax newspaper is printed on laser printers and reproduced on copy machines or even printing presses. It can also be received over the World Wide Web where it is available in Adobe Acrobat form.

MORE ON-DEMAND PRODUCTS

There is virtually no end to on-demand product types. Here are some other products that are well-suited for the technology:

- Envelope/packaging. Because of the unique creation and production requirements, we believe that digital printing has great applications in the production of packages. Many desktop digital printers now have envelope printing capabilities.
- Financial/legal. This category is composed of quarterly and annual reports, 10Ks, and investment/legal reports. Not unlike the brochure/booklet category, these can be produced on-demand.
- Invitations/menus. Invitations are relatively simple, but menus can be quite complex, but they both require very short runs.
- Letterhead/stationery. Letterheads and stationery consist of flat, single-sided pages. This category also includes business cards, tags, and labels, which I expect to include more color. One may view the machines in airports and malls, where they make business cards and stationery as on-demand systems.
- Newsletters. This is one of the most popular applications of desktop technology (books/manuals being first). Most newsletters have smaller-than-average run lengths, and are prime candidates. This has become a popular application for the Xerox DocuTech technology.
- Signs/posters. These products are categorized as display-oriented material and are characterized by large type sizes and increasing use of color. Digital printing is usually applicable up to 11×17 in., which covers a significant amount of single-sheet work.
- Books/journals. Journals may be more apt to go on the Internet or CD-ROM, but we envision a variety of approaches to on-demand book production. See the chapter on this subject.

The list that follows has over fifty products that lend themselves to on-demand printing. It continues to grow as early practitioners use the imagination to meet customer needs. The following chart shows the major categories of short-run printed products by primary application.

Data sheets	Stationery	Pre-prints
Menus	Fact sheets	Meeting notes
Reprints	Operating manuals	Product specifications
Book covers	Presentations	Greeting cards
Promotion sheets	Manual covers	Notices
Guides	Price lists	Record, CD, video covers
Newsletters	Organization charts	Counter cards
Packaging	Small journals	Directions
Folders	Instruction sheets	Posters
Maps	Conference programs	Flyers
Signage	Parts lists	Trade show handouts
Brochures	Art reproductions	Custom books
Package inserts	Personalized checks	Coupons
Real estate promotions	Labels	Sales letters
Retail materials	Catalog sheets	Forms
Direct mail	Wholesale materials	Custom catalogs
Invitations	Ads	Reports

INAPPROPRIATE APPLICATIONS

If you look at others people's lists of what you can do with on-demand, digital, or customized printing you almost wonder—what can't be done? Perhaps we should list those products that do not lend themselves to short-run approaches. The question was simple: what kinds of products would continue to require long runs? Here is my list:

- Consumer product packaging. Once past the design and testing phase, most mass-market products would require runs in the millions. Theoretically, you could make a case for regionalization of production or even smaller runs, but I just can't see packaging a few hundred boxes of Corn Flakes™, unless they were making a special run for you with kumquats and raisins.
- Metropolitan daily newspapers. Whatever you say about the newspaper industry, the metro daily will still be a mainstay, if

only to give commuters something to do. There will probably be fewer newspapers, but there will still be newspapers.

- Mass-market books. Certain authors and their books will be able to sell millions of copies in either hardcover or softcover form, and it makes sense to print in longer runs.
- Political and institutional fund-raising promotions. Blanket mailings to every home or selected homes are the only assured way of reaching a mass audience.
- Tax forms. Although the government will encourage electronic filing, the majority of taxpayers will not have access to the technology.
- Telephone books. Eventually, the cable system will link your telephone and television, and the directory will be electronic.
- Certain magazines. Many general and special interest magazines will still have vast numbers of readers for the print version, even if they offer an electronic version.
- Certain catalogs. There will be the need for mass distribution of certain consumer catalogs, especially if the products appeal to a large cross-section of the population.
- High-volume direct mail. We could make a case that even though it might not be delivered by the Postal Service, direct mail will exist for certain mass mailings, especially the ones that tell us that we could win millions of dollars.
- Promotional material. Brochures, flyers, and the like will be used by dealers and distributors that have products and services for a mass market.

There are probably others, but these came to mind quickly. Let us not assume that all reproduction will go short-run. It will certainly be digital, but run length depends on the audience.

8 BOOK PUBLISHING

Publishing books, like other niches in printing and publishing, is changing based on emerging technologies and ancillary production issues such as paper cost, inventory risk, and distribution costs.

Developing more efficient production methods for creating publications and more efficient delivery vehicles is becoming more and more important as publishers compete for consumers' attention with other media.

Due to the alternative production and distribution options, the methods used to prepare, create, and distribute traditional books created on an offset printing press using film-based prepress, stored in warehouses, and distributed with ground-based methods are currently under fire.

Traditionally, book publishing has been accomplished using offset printing with the run lengths based on estimated demand or cost efficiencies. Due to the costs associated with the printing process, especially the prepress and press makeready costs, publishers typically produce books in run lengths of 1,000–10,000 units. Once printed, the majority of the books are warehoused and distributed as demand dictates.

Alternative books would include CD-ROM, online, and books created on on-demand presses or digital color presses. With information content, teaching styles, and classroom demographics changing annually, can that stale old black-and-white textbook maintain its value as a teaching tool? Furthermore, how will it compete with color books or books on CD-ROM with interactivity and audio/visual capabilities?

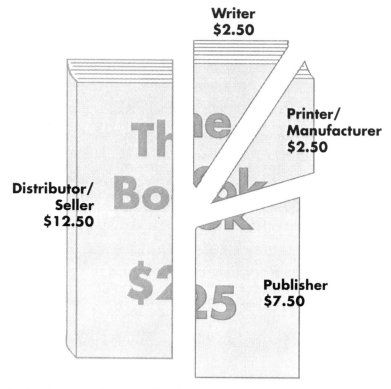

The distribution of the price of books.

ISSUES IN TRADITIONAL BOOK PRODUCTION

The traditional methods of creating books are costly because of the prepress costs, which include film, processing chemistry, and plates, as well as the time and cost of collating and binding. In addition, high costs due to setup and spoilage in both the press and bindery areas increase the costs of short-run books and first editions. This problem is most apparent in specialized academic and professional fields, where a popular title may only sell a few thousand copies.

Another expensive operation in book production is collation, which is the process of gathering the pages into the correct order. In book publishing it is often a greater expense to collate after the printing rather than before. This can add additional expense to the final price.

One factor particularly relevant to book publishers is the risk of obsolescence. This increases the advantages of on-demand printing. Textbooks used in high schools or colleges can become obsolete in only one or two years. For this market segment, producing textbooks on-demand would reduce costs and risks.

Obsolescence is an important word in book publishing. Obsolescence means that the product is no longer useful for the purpose for which it was created. Slowly, and over an extended period of time, what once was a timely and appropriate item becomes out-of-date and worthless.

There are different rates of obsolescence. Some books like *Tom Sawyer*, *Catcher in the Rye*, and *Treasure Island* may never lose their value. The content in these classics may never be altered. On the other hand, a large majority of books do suffer from obsolescence.

For these books the ability to update becomes very important. Any books that discuss technology require frequent updating.

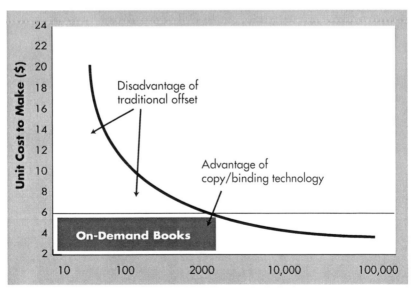

Comparison of cost per copy for short-run books.   Courtesy of Xerox

CUSTOMIZED TEXTBOOKS

For the 3,300 colleges and universities in this country, the costs of printing short-run documents has skyrocketed. Besides the course materials, these documents also include manuals, research reports, and alumni materials.

In addition, with the average publishing and production cycles ranging from 18 to 36 months, the textbook industry is hard-pressed to keep pace with the demand for rapidly changing information. This is most evident with areas such as computer-related or technology-driven research.

As a result, teachers are challenged to find current sources for classroom subjects and sometimes create their own course materials. These are customized materials compiled from chapters of separate textbooks, articles, essays, and other materials. Often, the issue in creating customized books is permission for the use of copyrighted material. As we will see in subsequent sections, these can be handled through college bookstores or off-campus copy shops. With the price of paper and printing rising, universities and other schools are challenged by several problems with course material. How do these institutions make their materials more timely, accessible, and affordable? In addition, schools are looking at ways of managing and customizing instructional materials. These institutions have begun to realize the potential for digital document management.

COPYRIGHT ISSUES

Kinko's Graphics Corp. lost a two-year battle in U.S. District Court in New York on March 28, 1991 when the judge found that Kinko's infringed on publishers' copyrights in selling photocopied course packets to students as study aids. The lawsuit was initiated by the Association of American Publishers (AAP) and eight publishing companies. The court ruled that Kinko's was infringing on copyright protections when its copying shops around the country sold excerpts from books to students without obtaining permission or paying royalties.

THE COPYRIGHT CLEARANCE CENTER

One possible solution is the Copyright Clearance Center in Massachusetts, which is becoming very active in administrating copyright issues for course pack materials at college bookstores around the country. Requests are growing in leaps and bounds. In August 1993 it handled 40,000 requests for copyright clearance of materials—an increase of 148% compared to 1992. In 1994 it distributed more than $2 million in royalties.

SUMMARY

In summary, on-demand, digital, and customized book publishing offer very powerful advantages over traditional book publishing. These advantages include:

- Short-run production—print only when you need it
- Reduction in inventory, inventory risk, and storage costs
- Elimination of obsolescence, because books are easily updated

These solutions can be utilized by various groups in our industry. Currently these groups include:

- Publishers who want to print books on-demand
- Campus bookstores or off-campus copy shops that create customized course ware
- Libraries to preserve and store books digitally instead of storing them on shelves or on microfilm

The benefits to customers include:

- Improved economies for short runs
- Fast response to customer orders
- Books will never become out of print because you can always print an original from the digital file
- Books would never have to be deleted from a catalog unless the content becomes obsolete
- Authors' proofs and review copies could be produced in record time

- Color pages can be "tipped in," and color covers printed on color copiers or other short-run methods
- Short-run books can be produced cost-effectively
- New markets can be reached through publishing titles not possible due to economics.

9 IN-HOUSE APPLICATIONS

One of the advantages of desktop computers and publishing is that the low entry-level costs made document creation and publishing more accessible for the masses. The masses ranged from students using Apple II computers to professionals working in-house centers preparing documents for printing.

Large companies depend on documents for everything. There are often large support systems supporting in-house authoring, printing, and distributing of paper documents. In many cases, they create the fabric of communication within a company. Besides their role in internal communication, many companies depend on document creation for advertising and documenting the completion of individual tasks (i.e., sales).

Traditionally, there have been three reasons to create an in-plant printing service—cost, control, and security. Recently, however, a new motivation has emerged, the motivation for inexpensive color documents in short runs.

COLOR DOCUMENTS ARE HOT

The use of internal color documents is increasing. A recent study from the Hewlett-Packard Company suggests that a majority of American corporations is moving to color printing. In the survey, 75% of the 400 MIS managers queried said that the businesses they support have acquired or plan to acquire color printing capabilities in the near future.

Eye-catching, internally-produced color is being used to call attention to everything from computer-generated designs to presentations and internal and external documents. If companies with internal color devices decide to increase the run length from a handful to a few dozen, then they will realize they need devices faster than the four-page-per-minute color copier.

CUTTING COSTS

In business today, everyone is looking for ways to cut costs and increase profitability. Almost everyday an article appears in the newspaper describing how companies are eliminating nonessential business services and costs in an attempt to increase cost-effectiveness.

Progressive organizations are building competitive advantages by delivering documents faster and cheaper. This ability increases sales effectiveness in indirect ways as well as direct ways, analogous to how reengineering increases productivity in direct and indirect ways.

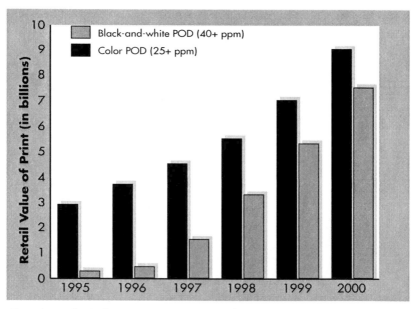

Growth market in-house.   Source: CAPV

Companies that utilize digital and on-demand printing are increasing the speed of communication. This improves the businesses' responsiveness, increases productivity, and lowers total operating costs.

The advantage of on-demand and digital color printing that makes it so attractive for in-house operations is that the information remains digital until the moment before it is needed on paper. This allows data to remain fluid and insures that the most current information is printed.

U.S. businesses spend over \$180 billion a year on printing. How much a company spends depends on the specific company, the product or service it sells, and the company's size. Studies show that the costs are much higher than companies estimate.

There are two factors commonly associated. One is the failure to recognize the total cost of production. Often, the corporate focus is on cost per page and not the total cost for delivering the printed piece. Factors often neglected include storage, retrieval, document tracing, shipping, disposal, and obsolescence.

The second factor is an inaccurate underestimation of the amount of printing done by the in-house operation. According to companies that specialize in in-house organizations such as Xerox and Interleaf, 90% of the printing in a company is done outside of the plant.

CONTROLLING MISSION-CRITICAL DATA

One of the most important uses of documents is for the communication of mission-critical information. Another way to discuss them is to categorize them as strategic. They may include new drug applications in the pharmaceutical market, product reference manuals in the high-tech industry, or product portfolios in an investment company. In contrast to office memos and database information such as bank statements, they are strategic because they contain the company's most critical information.

Documents that contain business-critical data are at the very heart of these business procedures. To take advantage of this asset, organizations are reengineering print production with document management systems that allow them to store, access, distribute, and manage documents efficiently.

Using traditional print production methods requires a long period of preparation and a hand-off from the document creator to the print shop for scheduling. After the hand-off, the print shop requires lead time for setup and print production. Printing business-critical documents on-demand decreases turnaround time, reduces cost, and increases timeliness.

With traditional copiers or offset printing, forms production is slow, costly, and complicated. Traditional copying methods using paper masters do not allow for easy revisions—a big disadvantage, since forms must be updated frequently due to changing government and insurance regulations. Long prepress setup times necessitate large offset print runs, forcing healthcare organizations to print more than they need, warehouse what they don't use, and throw away inventory when forms need revision.

Using on-demand and digital printing services, HMOs are creating an integrated system designed especially for the managed healthcare industry. It reduces the length of time necessary for gathering and organizing information for printing. It shortens the update cycle time by allowing electronic editing, compilation, printing, and production.

Plus, you can print the quantity you want, when you want, thus cutting the cost of production, mailing, inventory, and waste. The flexibility of this system helps reduce costly overruns by allowing you to print on-demand. Directories can also be customized to serve a targeted group of subscribers.

One major insurer already encourages its agents to create reports, direct mail, or other customer-oriented materials at a desktop computer and print them from centralized regional offices, transmitting files, complete with desired distribution lists, to the in-house printing system. Name and address data is merged with the documents to create personalized communication, and jobs are automatically output and mailed.

Using electronic job tickets permits individuals to specify finishing and delivery instructions directly into the job ticket without making a phone call or leaving their desks. As a result, productivity is greatly improved throughout the entire organization, not just in the central office. Using on-demand technologies allows insurers to adapt quickly and easily to changes, such as fluctuations in procedures, regulations, and premium rates. Traditionally, this would require additional print runs to constantly update training and procedure manuals as well as agent rate books. For insurers, traditional methods of print production are time-consuming and expensive. For them, on-demand technologies are more flexible. They can produce and distribute updated materials in days, not weeks, and forms can be revised and updated quickly and inexpensively.

RETAIL AND WHOLESALE APPLICATIONS

In the retail and wholesale markets, competition is at an all-time high. There is pressure to increase market share, revenue, and profits, to track buyer trends, to improve customer service, to establish strategic alliances, to build or strengthen value-added services, and to reduce costs. To answer these concerns, management is looking for well-defined solutions to their document management problems.

On-demand can help retail and wholesale companies improve productivity—not only in document creation but in facilitating decision making—by getting the right documents to the decision maker at the exact point of need. Well-integrated on-demand systems can eliminate steps in the offset production process and reduce costs and improve turnaround time, enabling them to respond to niche demands and better meet the requirements of customers and suppliers.

Downsizing or rightsizing has caused these companies to examine more economical printing technology. These companies, like others, have found that improving efficiencies in storing, distributing, and printing documents can increase productivity especially in the areas of forms automation and publications production.

SUMMARY

There are several good examples of in-house on-demand solutions that have been successfully applied such as financial and professional services, government, healthcare, forms management, and wholesale/retail.

Documents have an essential role in businesses that serve the financial and professional community, including insurance companies and banks. The documents created by these organizations are the vehicles for the services they provide to their clients.

Growth, combined with the rate of information change and the desire to keep consumers informed, has made it very difficult for organizations to create, store, and distribute up-to-date documents. The documents required are close to 100 billion pages a year. Of those, 10 billion are handled in in-plant agencies, and 60 million pages performed through outsourcing. As control and speed of delivery becomes more important, more corporations will bring these services in-house.

Forms printing is the largest printing application in the healthcare industry. For example, hospitals with 300 or more beds use 1,500–5,000 different forms. The resulting printing and publishing volumes per hospital can range from 280,000 to 900,000 pages per month. This is expensive and slow. Forms are either bought or produced in-house on offset printing equipment. Usually long printing runs are performed, and the forms are warehoused.

Since forms are constantly updated due to changes in governmental regulations, insurance policy changes, hospital requirements, and record keeping, the old forms become obsolete and are thrown away. Costs are increased as revised forms are printed and stored to replace the obsolete forms.

Although not discussed earlier, another application for this technology is for national, state, and local governmental agencies.

These agencies have diverse document requirements. As a result, often it is difficult to anticipate the number of documents required. For example, some issues generate great public and press interest and a concomitant number of documents while others do not. As a result, it is not uncommon to print too many documents, which are thrown out, or too little, which require additional printing.

10 THE ON-DEMAND MARKET

One of the forces driving the interest and excitement in on-demand, digital, and variable printing are market research reports. Although each company and study is different, they all come to the same conclusion—the market is growing, and growing fast.

A MARKET SUBSET

Short-run printing is a subset of the printing market in general. It is not that buyers want only short-run printing; they want printing, and some of it will be short-run printing.

We must do more to define what we do as an industry, not how we do it. We use the terms printing and copying without any thought as to what they signify. It is said that we define ourselves by our biggest machine, and that is a printing press. Copying involves machines that take an image and reproduce it without traditional plates or inks. Printing implies ink; yet, digital printers do not use traditional ink.

Our point is that there has always been a short-run, on-demand market. We applied copiers and electronic printers to that market, and will continue to do so. Now, however, we are applying specially equipped offset lithographic presses and a new breed of digital presses.

NEW TECHNOLOGIES SHIFT EXISTING METHODS

Studying past effects of new technology on previous communication methods, one thing becomes perfectly clear: new technologies change consumer demand and consumption. Let's use two examples—Automated Teller Machines (ATMs) and television sets (TVs).

It wasn't that long ago that you had to go to a bank (and only your bank) or the corner grocery store to cash a check and get money. The emergence of a new technology, the ATM, changed that. Today, it only takes a plastic credit card and a personal identification number (PIN) to get money at any bank in the United States or abroad.

This is a good example of how new technologies change consumer demand. Today, you probably would not even consider opening a checking account that could not be accessed by an ATM card. The new technology changed our demands. The same principles could apply to printing. In the future, one may not even consider going to a printer unless the printer can offer on-demand services.

Another example is radio, which thrived at one time and was once the communication medium of choice. When TV was introduced, however, it changed the way we used the radio. Most people don't sit around the radio after they get home from work—they turn on the TV set. The way we listen to radio or consume it is in our cars or at work. The new technology changed our consumption demands.

When existing research is examined and interpreted, it becomes clear that on-demand, digital, and customized printing and publishing are growing in importance.

THE FOUR ADVANTAGES OF ON-DEMAND

There are four main differentiating factors of on-demand products and services:
- Reduced cycle time
- Shorter run length
- Cost per copy of short runs
- Variable printing

For certain market segments, "time is money" more than "money is money." For these market segments, electrophotographic or toner-based on-demand printing technologies offer significant advantages. It is possible to walk into a facility using an on-demand press at 9:00 AM and walk out by lunch time with 50 or 500 impressions.

When the on-demand presses where first introduced into the marketplace, the run lengths were estimated to be between 35 and 5,000 impressions. Since then newer technologies have been introduced that compressed that market. On the high-volume end of the spectrum are the direct-to-plate-on-press options (Heidelberg Quickmaster, Omni-Adast), and plate and press enhancements such as automatic plate mounting.

On the shorter side of the market, the technological advancement shifting the minimum number higher is faster color copiers. As a result, the appropriate market today starts at about 50 impressions. Anything shorter could be done on a high-speed copier. On

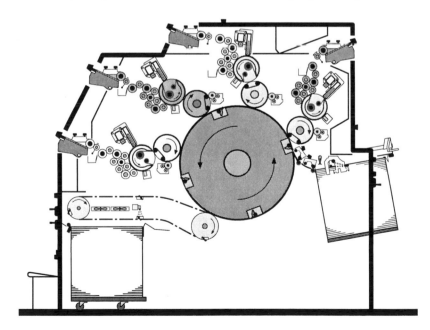

Schematic of the Heidelberg QuickMaster.

the higher end, the market has been reduced to 3,500, but most shops do not exceed about 1,000.

Cost is another differentiating factor. Imagine that you had to print one page off a press and had to stop that press and sell it, that one page could cost $10,000. If we print two pages they would cost $5,000/each, and three would cost $3,333/each. As the print run increases, the price per page decreases.

Copy technology on the other hand is different. If it costs $0.45 a page for the first page, it will cost the same for the second and third pages. If a client is paying $3.00 a page, copier-based technology is less expensive than traditional printing technology until a certain break-even point is reached.

As I discuss throughout the book, one of the strongest selling points of on-demand products and services is the ability to use variable information to customize and personalize the product and increase their sales effectiveness.

A question that I have posed to many market research firms is, how much variable printing is actually done? Since I have not discovered any reasonable methods of analysis, we estimate that only a small portion (about 1%) of the overall printing done in the U.S. utilizes this advantage. We are not really sure why variable printing is not catching on, but one possible reason is that the various software (i.e., database software) packages are fairly new.

THE FIVE SELLING FACTORS

In the last section we discussed the importance of understanding the benefits of the technology for the customer. The next consideration in the successful sale of on-demand products and services includes:

- Product positioning
- Promoting the benefits
- Reconsidering your contact
- Thinking creatively
- Overcoming buyer resistance

1. Don't position it as the same old thing. There was an effective advertising campaign a few years ago used to sell cars. It said "This is not your father's car." It was an effective selling tool because it drew a clear picture in the minds of the customers. This picture helped position and differentiate the purchase in the minds of the customers.

2. Learn and promote the benefits. To extend the analogy one more step, service providers need to present their "This is not your father's car" message to their market—clearly, distinctively, and efficiently.

- Don't just say that the equipment prints directly from diskette. Describe how the print runs can be shorter, for less money, and allow for more frequent updates.
- Don't describe the dots per inch, lines per inch, or levels of gray per pixel. Instead, discuss how a more targeted piece will cost less and result in a higher response rate.
- Forget about graphically showing how many steps have been eliminated. Sell the fact that, because of this, they can walk in the door at 8:00 AM with a job and walk out at lunch time with printed sheets.

3. Reconsider your contact. Many early users discovered that the person they sold traditional services to was the wrong person to sell on-demand services to. Get to the higher levels of the organization; to market to the marketers. These are the people who make the printing decisions, the ones who truly can understand the marketing potential of this technology. Others believe that it is the creative staff who should be the new contact.

4. Think creativity. The companies experiencing the greatest success are those that understand the advantages and figure out creative ways to use these advantages to benefit their customers.

5. Overcoming buyer resistance. One of the strongest motivations of on-demand printing can be a problem for first-time, non-risk-taking buyers. As discussed earlier, one of the greatest advantages is

reduced cycle time or fast turnaround, such as walking in the door at 9:00 AM and walking out at lunch time with 350 copies. There is no doubt that buyers must be comfortable with the procedure before they use it. Different companies use different approaches to overcome these concerns. Some offer tours and let customers watch production and talk to staff, and others offer seminars.

11 ACCEPTING DIGITAL FILES

Telecommunicating, or accepting customer's digital files over phone lines, is one way that service providers can differentiate themselves from the competition. In this chapter, we will discuss the critical importance of fast file transfers for on-demand printing, case histories demonstrating different ways to deliver the service, and the basics involving transferring and accepting files.

FILE TRANSFER FOR ON-DEMAND

As we have discussed in previous sections, one of the important, perhaps vital, motivations for on-demand printing is fast, convenient output. Anything that interferes with the delivery of fast, convenient products creates a significant hurdle in the delivery of this product. Therefore, the inability or time delay to get paper (as discussed in the paper chapter), a delay in delivery of the file, or late changes to that file would also create a problem.

Efficient file transfer solutions must be implemented by the printing company using on-demand printing technology. Of primary concern is that the file reaches the printing company intact and that the printing company makes it easy for customers to submit files.

As more and more company employees work out of a "virtual" office, which may be from their home office or from a notebook computer in a hotel room, the need for a wide-area network (WAN) becomes more important to the in-plant printer. A WAN, an extension of the corporate network, can use standard telephone lines to transfer data or can utilize higher-speed methods. Being able to accept files from detached customers is also a concern of the commercial printer, not just for on-demand printing.

The most common method of receiving files from distant customers is via "plain old telephone lines" (POTs). Using a standard modem to transmit files has been a common practice since the early days of computing. The speed of the transfer becomes important if either the modem speed is slow or the file size is large. Black-and-white on-demand printing usually generates relatively small files, normally around 1–10 MB. The current standard for modems is 28.8 baud speed, which translates roughly to 28,800 bits per second. If a 28.8 modem is used, a 10-MB file would take approximately 40 minutes to transmit. Transmitting files via modem is the most common method in use today because of the relatively low cost of the hardware and software.

Type of connection	Top speed	Text	Full-motion video
14.4 Kbps modem	14.4 Kbps	5 pp	0.6 sec.
28.8 Kbps	28.8 Kbps	10 pp	1.2 sec.
Digital (ISDN) phone line	128 Kbps	40 pp	5.0 sec.
T1 dedicated connection	1,500 Kbps	500 pp	60 sec.
Cable modem	10,000 Kbps	3,300 pp	390 sec. (3.5 min.)
Fiber-optic backbone	45,000 Kbps	15,000 pp	1,800 sec. (30 min.)

"Comparing the size of the pipe." The chart shows what each type of connection can transmit in one minute at top speed for both text and full-motion video.   Source: Rachel Powell Norton/Cyber Times

If faster transfer speeds are required, Integrated Services Digital Network (ISDN) can be used. With ISDN service, the higher bandwidth or speed allows a file to be transferred in less time. Because

ISDN is a "dial-up" service just like a conventional modem, it is also well suited for the on-demand industry, because it allows the printer or service provider to accept files from a multitude of different customers at different locations. ISDN is becoming commonplace in the printing industry, especially if the work is in color. Color files can become quite large, sometimes 50–300 MB in size. Because of deadlines, file sizes of this magnitude must reach the printing company quickly. In addition, the cost of transferring these files must be considered. Because of the complexity of installing and maintaining ISDN lines, several companies provide turnkey solutions.

When receiving files from a customer for the on-demand print industry, a simple method must be implemented to ensure that the file is received and that the customer's production requirements are understood. An electronic job ticket is highly desirable.

The simplest form of this is an electronic message that travels along with the print job. An electronic Bulletin Board System (BBS) is a common method that a printing company will implement to allow a customer to send a file and attach a message to it. A BBS also allows a customer to retrieve files from the printing company.

All a customer needs is generic communication software, a modem, and a telephone line. If a customer needs a particular print driver or a particular PostScript Printer Description (PPD), it may be available directly from the printing company via its BBS. The advantage to the printing company is that setting up a BBS is relatively easy and inexpensive.

A dedicated phone line is desirable so that the customer can access the BBS anytime of the day. However if the customer is making a toll call to access the BBS, long-distance charges will apply during the file transfer.

Another method for a printing company to accept files with a text message is to subscribe to a commercial on-line service such as America Online or CompuServe. Subscribing to either of these services will allow the customer to send files to the printing company's screen name or number and attach a message to the file. If the customer sends the file via an Internet account, the printing company will still receive the file. These commercial services provide access to the Internet. The advantage to these services is that it is almost always a local telephone call.

A printing company can subscribe to an Internet service provider (ISP) to simply have electronic mail (email) capabilities. This will allow them to receive files from a broad range of customers. Printing companies, especially on-demand printers, have started to have their own web pages on the World Wide Web (WWW). These pages not only serve as advertisements for the printing company but also allow customers to submit files easily. Some of the more outstanding pages also allow a customer to have a price for a printing job quoted.

12 BINDERY ISSUES

In an attempt to increase productivity in any form of manufacturing, the first step is to identify your bottlenecks and develop strategies that overcome or work around the bottlenecks. However, after you address your bottleneck, your overall throughput may only increase moderately because another previously masked bottleneck appears. You may be wondering what this has to do with print production and the bindery. The answer is that the increased prepress and printing capacity, resulting from technologies such as digital printing, direct-to-plate technologies, and on-demand printing, is shifting the bottlenecks away from the actual printing process to other places such as file transfer, order entry, customer service, and the bindery.

For years we have attempted to eliminate the bottlenecks in print production by focusing on the following areas:
- Manual stripping
- Electronic retouching, trapping, and imposition
- PostScript RIPs
- Press speeds

Now that these printing bottlenecks have been reduced and makereadies have been accelerated due to new technologies, the location of the bottleneck has moved. One of the new bottlenecks is in the binding and finishing of all these pages. In other words, the bottleneck in print production has moved from prepress and printing to the bindery.

Another motivating factor underlying the interest in the bindery is a renewed concern about employee safety and health, which has prompted new alternatives to replace lifting, cutting, and sorting. The tradeoff: employees could run the machines via keyboard rather than by hand.

And lastly, there is the realization that the bindery may be the most important part of the printing process. Why? Because if the pages are cut or bound wrong, it must be reworked from the beginning at very high cost. As a result of these motivations, new solutions are becoming available and a renewed interest is being focused on the bindery.

BINDING 101

The finishing of digitally printed products can be divided into two categories:

- In-line finishing, which can be considered automated since the finishing operation is either incorporated into the printing machine or can be conveniently attached to the print machine.
- Off-line finishing, which can utilize existing finishing equipment, is considered a separate operation from the printing of the product. In this case, the digital printing machine is used simply as a printing press.

The decision to use in-line or off-line finishing is based on the type of work to be produced, the present finishing capabilities of the print shop, and the possible need for high security, where the printing must remain within the physical confines of the digital machine.

Finishing a digitally produced piece can be as simple as a staple in the upper left-hand corner or as complex as an elaborately glued and folded mailer containing separate pages with tear-out perforations. Proper planning for the finishing operation, while important, is not as intricate as in the traditional lithographic industry. The main difference is the sheet size.

While a digital printing machine can usually image two 8.5×11-in. (216×279-mm) pages on an 11×17-in. (279×432-mm) sheet of paper, a lithographic press may be printing a 23×35-in. (309×889-mm) sheet of paper that contains eight 8.5×11-in. pages. The smaller sheet size, with its smaller number of folds, is easier to work with than the many folds of the larger sheet size.

The traditional lithographic press finishing operation usually produces large quantities of the same image. The on-demand digital printing machine has the capability of producing a different image on each sheet of paper. This leads to finishing operations not possible with conventional lithographic equipment. For example, each page can be personalized with different information such as a name and address for mailing purposes, or the pages of a catalog can be customized with products directed to the recipient. This type of printing poses a challenge to the finishing operation since there can be no rejects due to bindery problems. Careful attention must be paid to ensure that each piece, because it is unique, is properly finished and accounted for. Solutions are available that electronically scan pages as they are printed to verify that the page is indeed printed and in the correct sequence.

The simplest type of in-line binding usually incorporated into the digital printing machine is stapling. The staples are normally fed off of a large roll of wire, ensuring a large supply. The upper left-hand corner is the traditional placement of the staple. A variation of this is called side-stitching, where two or three staples are placed along the left-hand edge of a book. Side stitching gives the publication a more finished book-like appearance; however, the book will not lay flat when side stitching is used.

Another simple form of finishing is three-hole drilling for placement into binders. This is usually performed off-line using a wide variety of traditional drilling equipment. A variation of this is to use pre-drilled paper, which usually adds 1¢ to 2¢ to the price of the page.

Comb binding, which uses a plastic piece to hold the pages together, is used frequently. This type of binding has the advantage of being efficient for very short runs. The process of cutting the holes into the page and inserting the plastic comb through the book can be performed on very inexpensive tabletop machinery to produce a few books, usually in an office environment. For larger quantities, the process can be automated, with larger machines that can drill multiple copies. The plastic combs range in size from $\frac{3}{16}$–2 in. (5–51 mm), which allow the binding of up to 500 pages.

The combs are available in a range of colors to lend a more designed look to the piece. The advantages of comb binding are its simplicity, the option of incorporating a thicker, possibly litho-produced cover, the ability for the open book to lay flat, and the opportunity for the book to be reopened to remove or add pages. The drilling process can be integrated in-line into several digital printing devices.

A type of binding that is similar to comb binding is wire coil binding. The book must be punched in a similar way to comb binding, then a wire coil is threaded through the perforations. This process is used when a more durable bind is required.

Tape binding is a form of perfect binding that can be performed either in-line or off-line. A strip of flexible cloth tape that contains a heat-activated glue is applied to the edge of a stack of paper. The glue will dry or cure almost instantly as it cools, making this process ideal for the on-demand print industry. The tapes are available in many different colors. The Xerox 5090 and DocuTech series of printers incorporate tape binding in-line into their machines and can accommodate page counts from 15 to 125.

Several manufacturers make off-line machines that apply the cloth tape. The machines can handle book thicknesses up to 1.5 in. (38 mm), and some also allow the contents of a book to be changed by reheating the tape and swapping out pages. The cloth tape type of finishing is durable, giving a very high pull strength. Heavyweight covers, either produced digitally or on litho equipment, can be incorporated into a tape-bound book. Tape binding also has the ability to allow a book to open flat.

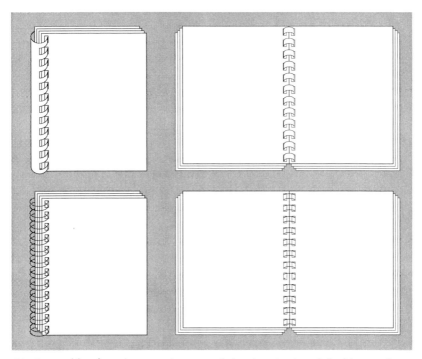

Mechanical binding devices: plastic comb binding (top) and double wire loop binding (bottom).

Saddle stitching is being performed on both in-line and off-line conventional equipment. With in-line saddle stitching, the pages are printed in the correct order until the book is totally printed. The collated pages are then stitched in the center with two pieces of wire, folded in half, and trimmed on the face edge. The entire process can be automated, with finished books coming off the end of the machine. The typical maximum page count is 88.

Depending on the thickness of the paper, finished trim size can range from 5.5×8.5 in. to 8.5×11 in. (140×216 mm to 216×279 mm). Some users choose to allow the digital printer to act as a printing press and then perform the saddle stitching on traditional off-line machinery.

In-line saddle stitching is growing in popularity. Since this is true in-line finishing, not only can each book have personalized infor-

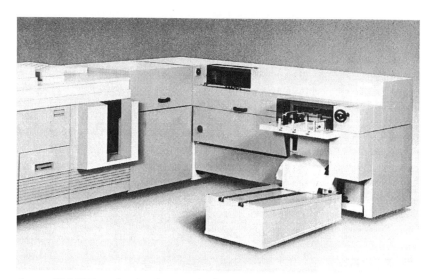

Bourg BB2005 perfect binder attached to a Xerox DocuTech.
Courtesy of C.P. Bourg, Inc.

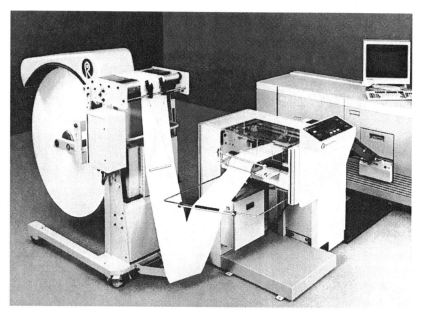

DocuSheeter™ , a roll-feeding system for the Xerox DocuTech and DocuPrint Publishing Series.   Courtesy of Roll Systems, Inc.

mation but the entire process can be automated. This is important for short-run, fast-turnaround type of work. Eastman Kodak and Xerox both offer in-line saddle stitching capabilities. If preprinted covers are needed, a cover insertion module available for the DocuTech will insert a preprinted cover automatically to the pile of interior sheets before the stitching process occurs.

A prime consideration when exploring the various finishing operations is the paper handling capabilities of the digital print machine itself. The number of different paper sources that a machine can utilize can be the difference between a fully automated system versus one that requires some manual assembly. Multiple paper drawers can contain different color stocks, or they can contain a front and back cover in addition to the white paper for the interior. This is a principal factor when producing manuals that will be three-hole-drilled. In addition to the white paper, there may be tabs, color sheets, or preprinted sheets. Having enough paper bins to accommodate these needs will allow a job to be fully automated without any manual collation needed.

Another concern with paper is how much the machine may hold. Having to stop periodically to refill paper supplies can slow productivity. An ample supply of paper, along with the ability of the machine to intelligently warn an operator when supplies are low is desirable.

13 DATABASE MARKETING'S ROLE

Another factor motivating interest in on-demand and digital printing is an emerging trend from marketers and retailers to better target their advertising dollars. Those who belong to organizations such as the Direct Marketing Association or believe articles in popular business publications (i.e., *Business Week, Forbes, Fortune*) talk more and more about the evolution of new marketing trends.

DIRECT

What's in Store for Stores

Donnelley poll examines retailer and manufacturer database plans

BY BETH NEGUS

president points out that it's not enough merely to *obtain* information, except-

Donnelley Mar-

Database Applications: 1994 vs. 1995		
Continuity Programs	'94	42%
	'95	68%
Consumer Research	'94	42%
	'95	68%
Customer Commun.	'94	42%
	'95	68%
Joint DB promo. w/ retailers	'94	16%
	'95	37%
Promotional Evaluation	'94	37%
	'95	53%
Intergrated Markting Comm.	'94	10%
	'95	25%
Media Planning	'94	16%

Cover story of Direct Magazine, August 1995, on the use of database marketing.

In the first trend, called "mass marketing," advertisers sent the same message to a "vast, undifferentiated body of consumers who received identical, mass-produced products and messages." This is often jokingly referred to by the Henry Ford slogan, "you can have any color car you want as long as it's black."

The second, more current trend, is to divide consumers into smaller groups with common demographics. Referred to as "market segmentation," the strategy was to divide anonymous consumers into smaller groups with common demographic characteristics to predict buying intentions. Using this approach, for instance, a 34-year-old married male, with two children, a house, and earning $50,000 annually would be a candidate for a mini-van advertisement because they are the segment of the population considered most likely to buy.

This hypothesis, that demographics predicts purchase intentions, is under close scrutiny. The evidence suggests that demographics do not accurately or frequently predict purchase intentions, but are more accurately predicted by previous buying patterns.

The latest trend, "database marketing," uses the philosophy that a more accurate indication of purchase intentions is based on what has been purchased in the past. This technology has become possible due to new technology that enables marketers and retailers to pinpoint smaller and smaller niches. These faster, less-expensive computers enable marketers to zero in on small niches of the population, ultimately aiming for the smallest consumer segment of all—the individual.

Marketers now closely monitor what we buy. This is evident in any supermarket that scans your purchases. They track what we buy, when we buy it. Although relatively new, organizations are now saving and sorting through this information, and more and more marketers are building databases that enable them to discern who their customers are, what they buy, how often they buy, and what they want.

For years, members of the Direct Marketing Association have advocated these strategies, and catalogers, record and book clubs, and credit card companies have successfully used these strategies to market their products and services.

These strategies are now moving into the mainstream. Today, companies ranging from packaged-goods to auto makers realize that in the fragmented, highly competitive marketplace of the 1990s, nothing is more powerful than knowledge about customers' individual practices and preferences.

If this marketing trend continues, traditional print production would be placed at a serious competitive disadvantage. In traditional print production, when 50,000 impressions are printed, they are impressions of the same exact piece. There is no unique message sent to an individual. Other forms of media, however, such as online services, can easily customize messages.

CUSTOMIZING TRADITIONAL PRINT

There are techniques available today that can customize traditional offset print. The two best examples are inkjet and Selectronic™ binding. Most of us have seen inkjet personalization. It has the ability to stop us dead in our tracks. Thumbing through one of your magazines, you notice something that catches your eye—your name printed on an ad saying "John Doe, this product is for you."

Selectronic™ binding is less obvious. A large automotive manufacturing company may buy a page in a popular magazine and advertise a convertible in the Florida version, and a sport-utility vehicle in the Denver version based on demographic information. Although inkjet and Selectronic™ binding are both available, they are only used by a small portion of advertisers. The first publicized demonstrations of inkjet personalization technology occurred at the Print 91 trade show in Chicago. Selectronic™ binding technology has been around for more than 15 years. Some of the earliest reports of the technology discuss how Donnelley used it in early in the 1980s. Today other printers such as World Color Press, Quad/Graphics, and Perry Printing have these capabilities.

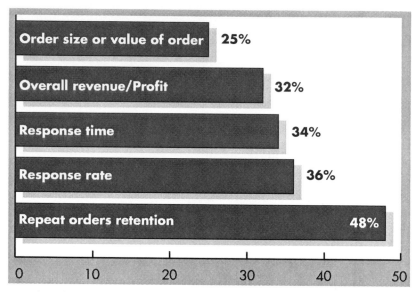

Benefits of personalization. Personalization can result in significant improvements in direct mail campaigns and promotions. Effective database printing results in an average 35% better performance, and a 25% improvement in average order size through cross-selling programs. Repeat orders and customer retention rose 48%. At the same time, overall revenue or profits increased 32% and response time improved 34%.   Source: CAPV

If database marketing and personalization are becoming more important, it is difficult to understand why inkjet and Selectronic™ binding have not grown faster. According to *Folio* magazine (Nov. 1, 1993) there are two reasons for the slow growth of Selectronic™ binding.

One problem with database-generated Selectronic™ binding is that in most fulfillment systems it tends to slow down the process. For example, if you want the bindery to insert certain pages into one magazine and withhold them from another, your fulfillment tape must contain complex instructions, which will ultimately slow down the equipment.

In addition, most fulfillment houses cannot process the load of data needed for individual customization, and therefore can't perform complex segmentations on their own. Although marketing databases do have that capability, they usually are not updated frequently enough to create weekly or even monthly tapes. Even if they are, there is often a time lag between the transmission from the database to the fulfillment file.

The most important factor, however, for deterring the acceptance of Selectronic™ binding is the fear that the technology will increase production costs. For those who are not leery of the price, there is the additional challenge of convincing advertisers to pay more. The publishers must decide if the additional costs can be offset by increased revenues from advertising and/or circulation.

For the most part, databases and publishers are not equipped to handle Selectronic™ binding. But, publishers are giving more attention to the technology due to demands from advertisers and the possibility of more effective promotions.

A black-and-white version of a color document that used variable information to customize brochures for sales representatives selling computer equipment. On the far left you can see the area in which the salesperson's name would appear.   Courtesy of Agfa, a division of Bayer USA

CUSTOMIZED ON-DEMAND PRINT

Utilizing on-demand printing, direct digital color printing, and database marketing, retailers can send consumers personalized advertising that targets the products or product categories they sell. Instead of getting a Sunday newspaper insert in which 90% of the products are not of interest to you, you will get an insert in which 90% of the products or product categories are of interest. In some ways, it could be the end of true junk mail. Lawn mower ads would go only to homeowners, and diaper ads would only go to parents. Combining on-demand printing or direct digital color printing would allow retailers to better target their products. Finally, an argument could be made that the ability to customize printed products might be the only way for print to remain competitive with emerging media technology. Remember, though, that most printing is subsidized by advertising. Without advertising, newspapers and magazines would not exist. Since advertisers have a choice of where to spend their dollars, they typically spend them in focused or narrow markets. When 500 television channels are available, retailers will have the ability to focus their advertising dollars to specific audiences more then they can today with print advertising.

On-demand printing, direct digital color printing, and database marketing, however, will allow print to be a more viable method of customizing and distributing advertising and will keep the printing industry competitive in today's cutthroat market.

THE FUTURE

The amount of purchases made through database marketing is minuscule in comparison to the amount of money spent in general retailing. According to *Fortune* magazine (April 18, 1994), Americans spent approximately $60 billion in 1993 through catalogs, TV shopping channels, and other direct-marketing alternatives. That only accounted for 2.8% of the nation's total annual expenditure of $2.1 trillion per year, however. Included in this figure are purchases made in supermarkets, mall outlets, car dealerships, department stores, warehouse clubs, boutiques, and other sources.

Marketers and merchants expect the amount of money spent through conventional retailing channels to remain steady or contract slightly as we approach the year 2000. Using new database marketing techniques, especially the customization and personalization features of the digital presses, database marketing should increase to 15% of total sales. With annual revenues of well over $300 billion, that would make database marketing one of the world's largest industries.

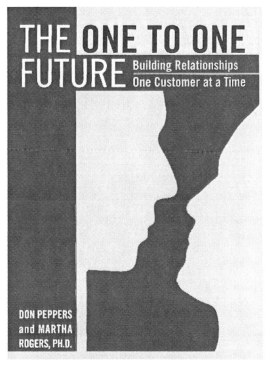

The One to One Future *is a good source of information about selling to individuals or the "market of one."*

14 OTHER FORCES OF CHANGE

Like other communication industries today, the publishing and printing industry is undergoing dramatic changes. The emergence of new technologies such as desktop computers and PostScript output devices combined with the increasing changes in print production, and environmental concerns, have contributed to a difficult period of transition.

Print customers have also heavily invested in desktop publishing equipment in order to send electronic files to their printers. Commercial printers have spent the last few years restructuring their businesses to meet the changing needs of their customers as a result. Today, printers receive more than 50% of their jobs in electronic form.

Other forces of change such as paper costs, postal rates, CD-ROMs, and a national preoccupation with online services have prompted print customers to investigate alternative production and distribution options. The methods used to prepare, create, and distribute traditional printed products are currently under fire.

A traditional printed product is one that utilizes plates, film, prepress, printing, finishing, warehouse storage, and ground-based transportation. Conversely, nontraditional or alternative products are those not requiring plates, film, long pressruns, warehouse storage, and ground-based transportation such as CD-ROM, online products, and materials created by on-demand, digital, and customized print.

New forces competing with traditional print, such as online services, CD-ROM publishing, and interactive TV have advantages as alternative products or alternative media. Once we define the advantages and disadvantages of traditional print and alternative products, we can figure out how print can compete in the new communications world order.

In assessing the advantages of different types of media we could discuss interactivity, attractiveness to advertisers, search and retrieval advantages, manufacturing cost, target effectiveness, and method of delivery—all relevant considerations in making decisions regarding which media will best suit your needs.

PDF-BASED PRODUCTION SYSTEMS

The high-speed data requirements of digital presses demand radical changes in RIP and workflow architectures. Developers are also trying to eliminate PostScript processing bottlenecks and accelerate deadline production times. In contrast with the bitmap or vector formats, the object-based PDF is slim and smart. Slim because, unlike the complex, continuous data stream in a PostScript file, it consists of a compact—or distilled—object-oriented database of imaging operations that can immediately represent the document, on a page by page level. Job ticket information, part of the PDF file, lets you store and manage device-dependent information, independent from job content.

The designer creates content using standard desktop publishing applications and converts it to PDF. This PDF digital master maintains the capability for viewing, proofing, and adding notes and edits to the file until it is RIPed. The service bureau or printer gets a self contained PDF file including all fonts and resources.

ONLINE INTERACTIVITY ADVANTAGE

The emerging vision of an online future in "cyberspace" has been the cover story of almost every popular magazine. Everyone from politicians such as Al Gore to the billionaire chairman of Microsoft, Bill Gates, have painted a detailed picture of future life online. Many people, especially academics, already work, shop, chat, and educate each other online. The future vision includes a new online realm that will put every conceivable form of information—from a newspaper or magazine to a digitized, interactive movie—online and available to anyone who has a computer and a modem. Millions of people collaborate daily on computer networks or log on to commercial online services to surf the Internet. Until recently, a select realm of universities and government agencies were privy to Internet access. New Internet service providers and new web-browsing software have emerged, making it possible for anyone to access the Internet. This big breakthrough began in 1993 with the creation of a subsection of the Internet called the World Wide Web (WWW).

The Web has two advantages: it is extremely user-friendly and is connected to other sites around the globe. Schools, government agencies, and businesses can build what is called a "home page." The home page can be thought of as a store front in a shopping mall. It uses a graphical user interface (GUI) so you can see "at a glance" what is on any home page and you can then decide if you want to see it or go somewhere else.

The other advantage is the linking or the "hyperlinking" ability. Unlike conventional online services such as America Online, CompuServe, and Prodigy, the Internet is made up of thousands of computers. With a web browser, which is software for the Internet, when you come to a word or sentence that is underlined or in a different color, you simply "click" on that area with your cursor or mouse, and you are instantly launched or sent to another computer that discusses that word or sentence in more depth.

While the Web is relatively new, it's the fastest-growing segment of the Internet. Web browsers such as Internet Explorer and Netscape allow you to interact with the Web sites and other Internet resources with point-and-click ease. In one stroke, the Web makes the Internet much easier to use and gives you the graphical tools to set yourself up as an information publisher.

All of this Internet activity has created a new communication medium. People looking for jobs are posting multimedia resumes to the Web, companies testing new marketing strategies are creating electronic storefronts, and even rock-and-roll bands like the Rolling Stones have a home page. Software, fonts, graphic images, and shareware can be downloaded from all over the world.

Underneath all of the publicity, the Web is nothing more than a set of hyperlinked elements that conform to a standard known as the Hypertext Markup Language (HTML). HTML is a subset of the Standard Generalized Markup Language (SGML), a standard for cross-platform publishing. SGML allows you to translate documents to other platforms and other media, such as CD-ROM. HTML, on the other hand, is not limited to text but can include audio, video, text, graphics, and tables, as well as links to resources like email, UseNet news, and other Web sites.

Earlier, we posed the hypothesis that if print production is subsidized by advertising, then advertisers will emphasize the medium that sells the best. Think about this—are online services a good vehicle for advertising? Better yet, are online services a good vehicle for selling?

ADVANTAGES OF SEARCH AND RETRIEVAL

It seems that whenever a seminar on new media is presented the publishers start wondering if they should start putting their publications on CD-ROMs. To answer that question, we should look at the advantages of CD-ROM and the publications that have fared best.

The greatest advantage of CD-ROM is that you can put a lot of information on them. CD-ROMs can store 650 MB without compression and 1.3 GB with compression. This translates to about 200,000 pages of text alone or five file cabinets of paper. A single CD-ROM can bring hundreds of thousands of pages of information to your screen, from entire encyclopedias to the complete phone directory of the United States.

But raw storage is practically useless without extensive searchability. This advantage is most clearly illustrated with reference materials such as a dictionary, encyclopedia, thesaurus, etc. The reason reference materials are selling well on CD-ROMs is because you can search the entire encyclopedia in less then one minute.

CD-ROMs have already vanquished one traditional market in the book publishing segment—the $700 million market for reference books like dictionaries and encyclopedias. Now, sales of CD-ROMs exceed those of the printed versions.

This trend is not new; in fact, it is several years old. According to an article in *Fortune* magazine published Oct. 19, 1992, reference works on CD-ROM were outselling their weighty counterparts an estimated 150,000 units to 100,000 units. Grolier's 21-volume encyclopedia on disk, weighs a paltry 0.6 oz., compared to the traditional printed version that weighs 62 lb.

The next target will most likely be the $9 billion market for textbooks and professional books. According to Nader Darehshori, chairman of Houghton Mifflin: "Within 20 years, most study materials will be computer-based, not printed."

ALTERNATIVE MEDIA-ONLINE

These advantages are not limited to CD-ROMs. Online services also offer interactivity and search-and-retrieval ability. Market projections show that the amount of money spent for online services is increasing. According to *Direct* magazine (Dec. 12, 1994), more than 61% of the 565 direct marketers polled said they will increase the amount of money spent on online marketing through such networks as Prodigy, America Online, and CompuServe.

Ironically, another use of online services is for marketing printed products. For example since 1992, readers have turned to On-line BookStore (OBS) for full-text, "distributive" Internet publishing of such titles as Nelson Mandela's autobiography, *Long Walk to Freedom* (in German and English), and Floyd Kemske's novel-in-progress about corporate takeovers and vampires.

The advantages of online marketing are not limited to commercial books. It is also becoming a force with college textbooks. Simon & Schuster Custom Publishing has created the "College On-line" interactive service. In this new electronic community, professors and students can:

- Interact on message boards and through conference rooms with others who share their interests
- Download supplemental course materials and software
- Search through information on Simon & Schuster's published textbooks and new media
- Benefit from author- and user-developed study tips
- Share information on various disciplines

Simon & Schuster Custom Publishing provides a variety of individualized publishing services to professors and students. Working with the Prentice Hall and Allyn & Bacon college textbook publishing groups, Simon & Schuster Custom Publishing offers college instructors the opportunity to create their own textbooks and course materials. Custom textbooks can contain material selected from Prentice Hall and Allyn & Bacon publications, as well as articles and readings from almost any source, professors' original material, students' essays, course syllabi, lab reports, and whatever else a course requires.

This is further evidence about the consequences of alternative media on book publishing.

COMMERCIAL ONLINE SERVICES

Most businesses have access to commercial services. Arguably, the best commercial service for business applications is CompuServe because of the comprehensive database services. One example is IQuest, a service that contains more than 800 publications and databases covering business, government, research, and news, and looks on other online services like NewsNet and Orbit. With an easy-find feature, locating articles and reports on any subject from several different sources is quick and easy.

Unfortunately, this is one of the most expensive services that CompuServe offers. One search costs $9, there is a $2–$75 surcharge depending on what databases are accessed, and retrieving an abstract costs $3. Theoretically, searching and retrieving one article could cost up to $100.

Fortunately, there are less expensive options. Depending on what kind of information you're looking for, you can often get it for a lower fee. Databases like Magazine Database Plus (Go: Database Plus) offer comprehensive lists of articles.

While the professional and expensive services on CompuServe may be too expensive, the basics provided give America Online and other online challengers a run for their money. For example, America Online with 3.5 million users is the fastest-growing service with a larger market share of home users.

SUMMARY

In summary there are new forces competing with traditional printing and publishing. These forces include CD-ROM publishing, online publishing, and interactive TV. These alternative media offer advantages such as interactivity, search-and-retrieval advantages, lower production and distribution costs, and marketing and advertising advantages.

On-demand printing and publishing are not traditional printing and publishing. In fact, we consider it a form of alternative media.

INDEX

ABOUT THE AUTHOR

Howard M. Fenton is a senior technical consultant/digital technology with the Graphic Arts Technical Foundation. The former editor-in-chief of *Pre* magazine, he is well known as a trainer, consultant, and speaker in print production. He has written over 200 articles, including a section in the *McGraw-Hill Science and Technology Yearbook* and scripts for the "Agfa Across America" educational seminars and PIA's PrintScan audiotape series. Fenton has also owned and operated a graphics company, managed a retail desktop publishing store, managed several prepress facilities, and taught computer graphics at Montclair College in New Jersey.

About GATF

The Graphic Arts Technical Foundation is a nonprofit, scientific, technical, and educational organization dedicated to the advancement of the graphic communications industries worldwide. Its mission is to serve the field as the leading resource for technical information and services through research and education.

For 75 years the Foundation has developed leading edge technologies and practices for printing. GATF's staff of researchers, educators, and technical specialists partner with nearly 14,000 corporate members in over 65 countries to help them maintain their competitive edge by increasing productivity, print quality, process control, and environmental compliance, and by implementing new techniques and technologies. Through conferences, satellite symposia, workshops, consulting, technical support, laboratory services, and publications, GATF strives to advance a global graphic communications community.

GATF*Press* publishes books on nearly every aspect of the field; learning modules (step-by-step instruction booklets); audiovisuals (CD-ROMs and videotapes); and research and technology reports. It also publishes *GATFWorld,* a bimonthly magazine of technical articles, industry news, and reviews of specific products.

For detailed information about GATF products and services, please visit our website at *www.gatf.org* or write to us at: 200 Deer Run Road, Sewickley, PA 15143-2600. Phone: 412/741-6860.

OTHER BOOKS OF INTEREST FROM GATF*PRESS*

- ***On-Demand Printing:***
  The Revolution in Digital and Customized Printing
  by Howard Fenton and Frank Romano

- ***Understanding Digital Color***
  by Phil Green

- ***Creating Your Career in Communications and***
  Entertainment
  by Leonard Mogel

- ***Careers in Graphic Communications: A Resource Book***
  by Sally Ann Flecker and Pamela Groff

- ***The Magazine***
  by Leonard Mogel

- ***Glossary of Graphic Communications***
  compiled by Pamela Groff

- ***GATF Encyclopedia of Graphic Communications***
  by Frank Romano and Richard Romano

- ***Handbook of Printing Processes***
  by Deborah Stevenson

- ***Screen Printing Primer***
  by Sam Ingram

- ***Flexography Primer***
  by Page Crouch

- ***Gravure Primer***
  by Cheryl Kasunich

- ***Lithography Primer***
  by Daniel G. Wilson

COLOPHON

The *On-Demand and Digital Printing Primer* was produced digitally as an on-demand publication. The text was created in Microsoft Word for the Mac, edited, and called into QuarkXPress. The line illustrations were created in either Adobe Illustrator or Macromedia FreeHand are in EPS format, and the photographs were scanned, modified in Adobe Photoshop, and saved in TIFF format.

The files for the cover were preflighted and imposed digitally two-up and then printed on a four-color sheetfed printing press. The QuarkXPress files for the book's interior were output as Adobe PostScript files, by printing to disk, and these files were used to print the interior of the book on a Xerox DocuTech 6180. The preprinted covers and the interior of the book were then bound inline to the DocuTech using the Bourg 2000 perfect binder.